D1528864

BREAKING PATTERNS

CATHERINE CHAPMAN PACHECO

BREAKING
PATTERNS

REDESIGNING
YOUR
LATER
YEARS

ANDREWS and McMEEL
A Universal Press Syndicate Company
Kansas City | New York

Library of Congress Cataloging-in-Publication Data

Pacheco, Catherine Chapman.
Breaking patterns : redesigning your later years /
Catherine Chapman Pacheco.

p.   cm.

ISBN 0-8362-2622-4

1. Middle age—United States—Psychological aspects.   2. Life style.
3. Retirement—United States—Case studies.   4. Aging—United States—
Psychological aspects.   5. Youthfulness—United States.   I. Title.

HQ1059.5.U5P33   1989   89-200

305.2'44—dc19   CIP

ATTENTION: SCHOOLS AND BUSINESSES

CONTENTS

CONTENTS

FOREWORD

In a recent television interview a vibrant septuagenarian actress was asked, "What are the benefits of growing older?"

"None whatsoever!" was her split-second reply, her tone implying that she wanted nothing to do with that tedious business of aging.

No one with a modicum of intelligence would choose to grow old; nonetheless, most people blithely surrender all the advantages of youth and sink without question into the stereotyped roles of the aged. For those who follow the opposite route, it is hard to understand how anyone could opt for old age's sickness, boredom, and societal rejection while forfeiting youth's health, zest, and Life with a capital *L*.

The multitude of individuals who are labeled by the world as old, but who are still jogging in marathons, scaling mountains, crossing oceans—in fact, engaging in all manner of exciting physical, emotional, and intellectual ventures—are a good indication that *age does not have to determine one's activities*, and furthermore, that for every person who is living by that truth, there must be a lot of others who are following the popular downhill route simply because they choose to do so. There are Pattern Breakers everywhere of many varieties—those of heroic travels and exploits and a large number of imaginative stay-at-homes—whose manifest well-being is providing a startling piece of news: *a person's activities can largely determine what his or her effective age will be.* So, since exciting patterns keep us young, and monotonous ones make us old, it is only common sense to make a daring break with all those damaging life-styles, take a giant step into new and challenging ones, and set all that rejuvenating excitement to flowing.

Many of those youth-inducing patterns—some oriented to distant and exotic settings, and others to the familiar hometown ambience—are explored in this book for the prospective Pattern Breaker's benefit. They are illustrated by anecdotes and examples taken from the offbeat life I share with my husband aboard our sailboat Romany Star, as well as from the lives of land and sea adventurers we have met along the way. It is important to note that although the need for calculated pattern breaking increases as the years go by, this is not an undertaking reserved for the chronologically older sector; everyone, regardless of age, will benefit from this imaginative approach to getting the most out of every day. Successful pattern breaking involves abandoning a negative situation and taking a courageous leap into a beneficial one; leaving a good pattern for a more desirable one, or for the sake of variety, exchanging one good pattern for another. A "good pattern" is not simply an enjoyable activity or hobby; total immersion in a new attitude toward life is happening, and the Pattern Breaker who evolves from this process defies categorization—by years spent on the planet or by any of the other standard ways of neatly filing people.

Although the boating scene is most certainly not the place for everyone, potential Pattern Breakers who feel the least bit insecure about making radical changes in their life-styles should find the description of my experiences helpful; techniques I used in order to gain the courage to change are included. It would have been hard to find a more unlikely candidate than myself for life aboard a thirty-eight-foot sailboat. Not only had I been severely handicapped for as long as I could remember by a water-related phobia that made me uneasy even when sitting on a snugly docked vessel, but I was also firmly ensconced in a comfortable existence that was the complete opposite of my present routine, which includes such novel features as continual movement of our living quarters, incredibly few square feet of indoor space in which to do everything that requires complete privacy, and most extraordinary of all (in my opinion), when away from marina facilities, a cockpit shower arrangement, which my husband can use in a standing position, but which I, for reasons of pectoral modesty, must use while kneeling. Nevertheless, this thoroughly unorthodox life-style has provided Tom and me with the most exciting segment of our entire thirty-eight-year marriage, and after nearly a decade afloat we continue to reap the invigorating benefits of daily exposure to challenge.

Since the sailing life is virtually without walls, we conduct our day-to-day activities in a way that is remarkable not only for its adventure but also for its vulnerability to people. Perhaps the most rewarding facet of our open, informal mode is the fast gut-level contact that we experience with all kinds of Pattern Break-ers—land dwellers who make sailing to different ports eminently worthwhile, and seagoing folk who form our everchanging "community."

My decision to write *Breaking Patterns* came as a direct result of this unremitting exposure to unusual men and women. Over the years I have been intrigued by the similarities that surface in the personalities of these innovators: their verve and acuity, their resoundingly good health, a sexual aura befitting persons many years younger than they . . . in short their overall failure to fit into their chronological age group. I decided long ago that they are worth imitating.

When Tom and I broke out of the mold—a mind-blowing change from retail executive and wife to gung-ho live-aboard sailors—we began a learning process that gathers momentum every day as we discover how to reject in a flash any practice that sows the seeds of aging, and how to always be ready to pack up and leave, with no regrets, a life-style that does not provide an experience of renewal, i.e., rejuvenation. For us the boating environment has proved to be the perfect field for staying young, but the world is full of other fields, and the potential Pattern Breaker's own abilities and desires should be the guideposts for determining the direction in which the first big move should be made. Good patterns—whether good marriages, friendships, habits, and hobbies—should be kept, serving as major threads in the tapestry of the new life. But Pattern Breakers should be ready to run, not walk, away from any situation that implies decline ("I need a one-story home because I'll probably have trouble going up and down stairs when I'm a bit older"), that overemphasizes physical or emotional security ("I have to live near relatives and longtime friends so that they can help me with illness and other personal problems"), that overemphasizes financial security at the sacrifice of life experiences . . . in short that carries any connotation contrary to vital participation in the world around them. In this book Pattern Breakers who retire are called Recommencers, for the simple reason that the vital lives they are leading should not be associated with a word that evokes thoughts of withdrawal and inactivity; these energetic people *are* recommencing, and this time they know how to do everything better.

When life becomes too secure, too easy, too much of an unbroken continuum of old patterns, with the past pouring into the present, and the present into the future with no major shifts in course, too many follow the direction they have witnessed in others who have plodded or coasted along similar time-worn ruts: they grow old . . . inexorably old. On the other hand, if every phase of life serves to challenge and excite, if we are willing to smash to bits a number of major old patterns and adopt some radically innovative ones, we will find that our minds are sharper, our bodies are stronger, sex is better, life is remarkably sweet . . . and we're young.

ONE

TAKING A GIANT STEP

A full-scale garage sale, with a typical complement of milling bodies and whoops of discovery, was under way in the incongruous setting of our condominium apartment. The carpets I had broken my back to keep in pristine condition were being trampled unfeelingly underfoot and were, after two days of this thorough abuse, candidates for steam cleaning. Cigarette stubs were squashed in my kitchen sinks, with the concomitant pall of smoke lurking ceilingward and into the tucks and folds of draperies. Babies and small children abounded. They were either sleeping or screeching, zonked out in strollers in lopsided rejection of this bizarre event or wheeling recklessly about the room and posing a threat to everything in sight.

A young woman togged out in blue sateen shorts, a tight knit shirt and jogging shoes, a wet trough between her shoulder blades, indicating that she had fitted this experience into her fitness routine, plucked one of my thirty-year-old Waterford goblets from a table, held it critically up to the light, then stashed it again among its sparkling siblings with what I interpreted to be a deprecatory shrug. Beside her a pair of chattering mothers rummaged through my best china, a complete service for twelve, generating a din of clacking and crashing sounds as they checked through the stacks of gleaming silver-rimmed dishes, crassly barging down what was for me a memory lane of warm and happy times with friends and family around the long mahogany dining table.

The dining table was conspicuous by its absence. Our apartment had been sold completely furnished, with the exception of the table. Thinking that one of our children—two sons, recently out of college—might someday want to possess a reminder of those good old family days, we had shipped the heavy piece of furniture, at a cost that must have outweighed its value, to my sister's home for storage. (Now, eight years later, it still occupies a prime spot in her basement, in dusty witness to the fact that parents and progeny can be miles apart when it comes to defining sentiment.)

As my motley clientele pressed from room to room, I knelt tiredly in the entrance area adjoining the living room, answering questions, sometimes collecting for a purchase, and in between, finishing the packing and addressing of several large boxes. These boxes were lined up in front of me, presenting a cardboard line of defense between those things that were expendable after three decades of accumulating and those things that represented, as it were, the essence of our marriage—nonnegotiable . . . not for sale. One group of boxes would be stored with my sister and mother; others would be mailed to our sons; and the remainder would go with us into our new life.

Heading the list of survivors to be stored was a carton of family pictures. Next in line were boxes with important papers and documents, such as our wedding certificate and several years' tax records; an alarming number of special school papers and childish art efforts; a yellowing assortment of baby clothes of two-decade vintage; a few favorite toys that might be enjoyed by grandchildren someday; some gifts that were not to be sold or given away, such as a set of kitchen implements with carved wooden handles, which had been purchased with our older son's paper-route money, and a tiny stick encrusted with "jewels" and painted with red hearts—a Valentine to me from our other offspring, then eight years old. Alongside my weary form were two clumps of objets d'art, as well as a number of things of purely nostalgic value, carefully mulled over and selected for each son. These awaited packaging and mailing. And just beyond, the biggest pile of all leaned precariously against the wall: linens and kitchen gadgets, dishes and utensils, to be boxed and shipped to the Virgin Islands.

To the casual observer the scene was not without pathos: this tired-looking woman crouched in a corner of her already-sold apartment, shuffling through her baby pictures as she compartmentalized her life and divested herself, it would appear, of her most valuable possessions. Looking more closely, the observer might even notice her occasional wince or grimace when those rows of tables of items for sale were rattled or banged against. And without question, there was a sentimental last look on her part as the Lladro figurine was borne out the front door, to be followed by the shapely crystal liqueur decanter, a silver serving dish, and the best little electric coffee maker for miles around. The uninformed would be forced to presume a financial disaster, possibly combined with a tragic divorce.

But ah! If they had only known! Tired, yes . . . sentimental, that, too . . . but the overriding feeling was one of exhilaration, pure and sweet. Tom and I were headed for a new life the pluses of which far outweighed memorabilia and other collectables. And we had chosen to go into that new life as unencumbered as possible.

The rewards that resulted from this giant step toward physical and emotional freedom proved to be beyond our expectations. As we proceeded to shed ourselves of the rooms and closets of objects, and of the thoughtfully decorated and tended apartment, we became increasingly excited over our new mobility—strongly reminiscent of those carefree years before we became "responsible people." The overall feeling was one of youthfulness; the accumulation of all those possessions seemed somehow synonymous with the accumulation of years. This emotion, incidentally, has stayed with us throughout the past eight years. We haven't regretted having sold or given away a single item, and when we travel—by plane, car, or sailboat—we travel light. There's no room for excess baggage in our new way of life.

To make this transition from an ambience of commitment and tradition to a world of personal liberation and keen expectancy—as some major old and ingrained patterns are literally smashed to pieces, and as a life-style is visually trundled out the front door—the individuals involved must have their eyes set on a sensational adventure . . . something they truly long to do . . . something so exciting that the mere thought makes them breathe a little faster, plants a sparkle in their eyes, makes them feel as young as anyone in the world who has ever set out on a rousing quest. And in that regard we certainly were not lacking. In a tranquil little marina in the British Virgin Islands, our future home was gently seesawing in its webbing of dock lines. We had painted the name Romany Star in large black script on the bow of our beloved Ohlson 38 sailboat and had spent the past three years preparing her and ourselves for the day when we would live aboard her and adventure to distant ports. With so much lying ahead of us, how could we be interested in looking back?

Only a fool would suppose that sailing and living aboard a vessel that is only thirty-eight-feet long and ten-feet-three-inches wide is meant for everybody. We can be as sybaritic as anyone alive, and there are many drawbacks and compromises in a daily routine that includes, among other singular features, cooking in an area where the icebox (not refrigerator) lid constitutes a major part of the counter space; often having to cook while sailing, strapped in so as not to topple over with the heeling and pounding of the boat; always having to be extra careful not to waste water; and, what is to the majority of people the most discombobulating necessity of all, having to manually pump out the head. However, the personal rewards from the life we lead make all the drawbacks seem unimportant; our pleasure comes from the fact that we love the ocean, the people we meet, the air of excitement that always prevails around boats. It is important to note, though, that this is *our* scene . . . what *we* like to do. The same degree of thrills, and just as many challenges, can be found elsewhere. The world is full of zestful life-styles to be tried on for size . . . thoughtfully experimented with . . . rejected . . . adopted.

And the key to the whole process of progressive rejuvenation appears to lie in our willingness and ability to smash old patterns to bits and pieces, and to reject anything that faintly resembles a standard continuum with negative, downhill implications—to wit, grandma and grandpa dedicating their remaining years to an enactment of the "over the river and through the woods" scenario. Far more inspirational for their descendants are grandparents who continue to live with youth and verve till the end of their lives . . . who show by what they're doing that the world is their oyster, too . . . who flatly refuse to be confined to any prototypical life-style that bears overtones of decline.

Whether the new life is to a boat, an RV (recreational vehicle), a farm, a house or apartment abroad; to college or an innovative business venture; or to any one of a multitude of unusual modes that stay within the old, familiar setting (the most challenging way of all), the important elements are to take that first giant step, to exercise great care that an old rut isn't being exchanged for a new one, and to always be ready to break patterns—even on a day-to-day basis. Youthfulness appears to lie in a willingness to make drastic changes and in a refusal to be typed. With this in mind, Tom and I refuse to confine ourselves to what is, for us, a paradisaical life afloat. Certainly, it is an especially varied mode, within which we can continue to break patterns. We are meeting new people as we cruise to different areas, and combining a number of interesting activities on land with our boating life. Exploration of the various communities to which we sail can be very rewarding, since we make friends among the citizens of diverse cultures, explore natural surroundings, stay as long as we like, and then sail on. Nonetheless, there are many other things we plan to work in around our life aboard Romany Star: for example, taking an in-depth look, via RV, at North America; living ashore for several months at a time in small-town settings in foreign countries (great financial strategy), and somewhere along the line, learning to raise our own food.

Adventurers, we have found, are really not so very different, at the core, from the general stay-in-the-rut population. By the same token that age doesn't have to determine one's activities, and that, instead, activities determine age, we have found that challenging activities turn the ordinary clerk, mechanic, and executive into brave people. Originally, they had to have the vision to break with the mundane, but it is the day-to-day challenge of the lives they lead that molds them and sets them apart. Broken down into laboratory specimens, so to speak, we would find that they really aren't Goliaths . . . they are simply people who exercised their right to break major patterns.

A good example is a late-fortyish couple we met on a trip to Puerto Rico. The husband, a physician, had exchanged a life centered around work and golf in the Chicago area for a job as supervisor of a small hospital on the south coast of the island; as a trained nurse the wife occasionally did volunteer work in various health programs. The couple's circumstances were still very comfortable, including a large residence and a household staff, but in terms of total income and the type of cultural environment they had always enjoyed—theater, art galleries, opera—a country town in Puerto Rico was at the other end of the spectrum from Chicago; likewise the doctor's new working situation was quite primitive by comparison with the large, modern Chicago hospital. They had taken the first giant step. Their reasons: "We wanted to do something different. When we looked at the retired people who had followed the groove we were in, we didn't like what we saw."

We maintained contact with these interesting people, and over the years they continued to break patterns. Their experiences in Puerto Rico made major changes in their thinking, and after a few years in that assignment, they moved to the U.S. Southwest and opened a small nonprofit clinic for the indigent. Our friends admit that it is unlikely that they would have taken that first giant step from Chicago to the nonprofit clinic. What they were doing in the time between the first move to the comfortable, yet more challenging life in Puerto Rico and the move to a decidedly more demanding pattern in the Southwest had revolutionized their outlook on the world and had turned them into truly brave people.

Another example of the fact that *we are or we become what we do* can be found in a middle-aged couple we met in St. Thomas who had somewhat miraculously inherited a boat from a distant relative of the husband. Back in the States they had both been school teachers and had never even day-sailed. But in the process of taking care of the new property, with the idea of selling it, they began to spend more and more time at the docks, and over the course of a year or so, became deeply involved in the sailing world. They began to think of themselves as sailors . . . wore nautical-looking clothes . . . regaled their students with tales of their weekend sallies into the ocean. The last we heard of this completely transformed pair, they were in the Pacific on the first leg of a circumnavigation.

An adventuresome mid-sixtyish couple we met during our days in the rat race—when my chief goal was to be the ideal executive wife—had left the whirl and intrigue of the cosmetic industry in New York to settle down in a condo on the west coast of Florida. The radical twist in their recommencement (i.e., retirement) was their fresh approach to their new life, along with the changes that this new life had obviously made in them. We met them at dinner at their son's home, and my first impression was that they had a far more vital bearing and outlook than our hosts or any one of the several dinner guests. Our friend's mother was attired in a flowing garment that swirled expressively about her compact little figure as she moved and gestured while describing to all these staid, stick-in-the-mud people how she and her husband had gone about recommencing after thirty-odd years in the marketplace.

"We decided that we wanted entirely different surroundings," she explained, "with everything new to go with our new life." Every item they owned—silver, crystal, china, and furniture—was given to their children or sold, and they furnished their condo apartment in ultramodern fashion. (The entire assemblage, including ourselves, was stunned by this daring move.) And though they loved their new life-style, which included a whole new group of friends and a small camper for exploring the surrounding countryside, these two were just beginning to break patterns. After two years in the apartment they were already planning to rent it out, then travel to a low-cost area of Spain and rent living quarters there, as a base for getting to know Europe. Their plans were financially sound. After airline fares and other expenses of locating in Europe, they would still be ahead, due to the favorable position of the dollar, and other factors. And it was clear that there would be a lot of other moves in the future; the sky would be the limit for this couple.

Adventurers that are made, not born, may have few more convincing cases in point than my own. Because of a number of traumatic incidents in my childhood, I had been burdened for as long as I could remember with an unreasoning fear of the water—indeed, with a full-fledged phobia. Despite Tom's utter ecstasy when in contact with the ocean, I had successfully managed for the first twenty-five years of our marriage to steer my steps in other directions. In fact I could seldom be induced to even go to the beach, owing to fear that I would be wheedled into stepping into the surf. Outings on boats were the last things on my list of possible activities, and if ever forced into sitting on a boat at anchor or—believe me, it's true—at a dock, I insisted on wearing a life vest. When induced to enter a swimming pool, I stayed at the children's end, next to the wall, and if Tom succeeded in leading me into waist-deep water, I would suffer choking, claustrophophic feelings. A far cry from the woman who now enjoys living on a boat . . . diving and snorkeling almost every day when at anchor . . . cruising away from sight of land for days at a time . . . doing night watches in heavy seas while Tom rests or sleeps below!

My decision to break away from the crippling pattern of fear resulted largely from the convergence of several events: our sons had moved away from home, and it was clear that my child-rearing days had ended; retirement was not too far in the future, and the prospect was prompting a good deal of self-examination; my husband had bought a Sunfish, a small sailboat, and was returning from weekly sessions with it all aglow, appearing ten years younger; several of our friends had gone into sailing small boats, and I was sitting on the fringes of all this nautical flurry, feeling like the proverbial lump on a log.

I knew it would be hard to overcome my fear of the water, but the alternative—a retirement consisting of little that was new and challenging—was too dreary to even contemplate.

The Sunday afternoon of my biggest breakthrough in the battle against fear is still a vivid memory. I believe it illustrates that what is largely involved in having the courage to break old patterns, even the pattern of fear, is a strong motivation toward what lies on the other side of the hurdle. Sometimes we think we want to make a change when, deep down, we prefer the status quo. To foster my soon-to-be-brave persona, I had forced myself to go sailing with friends a few times, on twenty-five- to thirty-foot boats. I had even gotten to the point where it was possible to go into the water of a peaceful bay with a life jacket on . . . as long as I was holding onto the ladder of the boat. On this special day we had been invited for an afternoon sail, and as we drove down the hill overlooking the marina, the whitecaps were making an angry froth of the water we were to sail through, and the boats that were already under way were heeling sharply under the stiff wind.

Tom gave me an "out." He said, "We can do this some other time. We'll have lunch at the marina and then drive back home."

The steps I had already taken had changed me to the point where I was able to reply, "No, I want to go out today." I knew that a turning-back that day would mean the end of my attempts to conquer fear. We set sail with the "patient" strapped into her perennial life vest. I even handled the tiller for a few minutes, and the exhilaration of this victory gave me my most significant push toward the eventual conquest of fear. Although my struggle was not wholly won for several more years, the prime negative pattern was dislodged that Sunday afternoon, and consequently, every step forward made me able to take the next step. I was being changed by the very process I was programming for myself. I was beginning to think like a sailor and act like one, and along the way I was acquiring all the courage I needed in order to be one. An entire view of life was being cast off, and another vastly more rewarding and fulfilling one was being acquired.

On a scale that may involve less trauma, this is precisely what can happen to anyone in the world who wants to do anything that appears alien to his or her usual way of life. The more difficult the change, however, the more piquant are the rewards.

Rewards become an everyday matter for Pattern Breakers. Day-to-day living becomes as joyous as vacations used to be for the man or woman who indulges in that wild creative urge that was suppressed because it didn't earn enough money . . . returns to school at an age when such a step is novel . . . opens a business for the sheer enjoyment of the experience . . . leaves white-collar work to become a mechanic because that was what he or she always wanted to do . . . changes from mechanic to white-collar worker, for the same reasons . . . moves to a foreign country, learns the language, experiences the culture . . . roams the United States, Canada, and Mexico by any of a wide number of transportation modes. The important thing is to get going—whether the adventure is physical, emotional, intellectual, or all three—to break those monotonous patterns and dare to do and be anything.

A sailing trip from Montserrat to St. Martin, both in the Leeward Island chain, stands out in my memory. The passage took a full day and night, and the weather was spectacular—sparkling blue seas and skies melding into a gorgeous sunset, then into a velvety, star-sprinkled night. Tom was resting below as I stood the eight-to-midnight watch. Our self-steering device was engaged, but as the wind shifted, minor changes had to be made in the pulleys that worked the tiller. Every ten minutes I would stand up and make a 360-degree inspection of the darkness, checking for ships that might be approaching our path. After one of these visual searches I stood for a while with a foot on either cockpit seat, holding firmly onto the mahogany boom gallows.

Romany Star's white sails gleamed dimly in the starlight, filled to nigh bursting with a fresh wind coming from abeam. Over the side I could see the phosphorescent glow from the path we were cutting through the waves. Around me, like jewels in an oceanic crown, shone the loom of lights from the islands of St. Kitts, Statia, St. Bart's, Saba, and St. Martin.

As we flew through that matchless night, another journey came to mind—a journey from a life handicapped by fear and phobia to one with limitless possibilities. The same woman who had felt nervous while sitting on a boat at dockside was now, only a few years later, handling this vessel while her husband slept below . . . was not afraid . . . was reveling in the taste of salt, the rush of wind against face, the rhythmic rise and fall of the boat making its way through the waves.

As I returned to my warm huddle in a protected corner of the cockpit, a sobering thought occurred: Had it not been for a decision to break the old, debilitating patterns and search for new ones, I could easily have missed this night . . . I could have missed it all.

REJECTING
THE EASY WAY

Life was becoming incredibly smooth. Tom was enjoying his job as a merchandiser and buyer and in the past few years had received a number of satisfying raises and commendations for his efforts. In my spare time, when I wasn't preparing dinners or parties for my husband's business associates or our fairly large circle of friends, I was doing research articles for a business publication, shopping with friends, doing a bit of volunteer work, and indulging as often as possible in delicious post-lunch naps.

Our sons had finished college and had started their respective careers as lawyer and as musician. Their belongings had been largely moved out of their closets to the distant cities where they had located, and their rooms had been earmarked for their brief visits home and for the many guests we would be inviting to share our golden years. In fact the apartment seemed suddenly overflowing with rooms of every kind: a study that looked awkwardly neat without its usual piles of college textbooks and term papers, a living room that was always perfectly tidy, and a dining room with a table that any number of dinner guests didn't seem to properly fill. A happy note on this deserted scene was our new financial status: with the drainpipe from our pockets into the university bursars' plugged for all time, we found there was whatever we needed for dining out, entertaining, doing most anything our modest appetites called for.

The first hole in the dike that surrounded our placid existence appeared in the form of Tom's sleek little Sunfish sailboat. It was hard to understand why he needed an activity so foreign to our land-bound existence, although I should have noticed years before that this patient man, saddled with a wife who abhorred the water, was being drawn unalterably toward a deep relationship with the sea. His love for the beach and his unflagging efforts to take me along should have told me something. During those first months with the Sunfish he would burst into the apartment, cheeks shining, tracking grains of sand, and smelling of salt, to regale me with tales of tacking, beating, capsizing, and righting, and to generally overwhelm me in my slothful, home-bound condition. Something big was happening to my husband, and I was not even a tiny part of the event.

The decision to overcome my fear of the water was the only feasible path. The alternative to this sudden split in interests—to ask Tom to give up his mad adventures on the water and join me for a tour of an art gallery—just didn't wash. In addition I could see him growing younger before my eyes. Sex was fantastic after these boating escapades, and with retirement age right around the corner, potions and aphrodisiacs of any kind were not to be disparaged.

As my personal battle against fear got under way, and after several months of showing some signs of progress, we graduated from day sails with forbearing friends—who didn't give in to impulses to push this pallid, trembling woman overboard—to the purchase of a twenty-six-foot sailboat of our own. Tom had sold the Sunfish, since it was a bit too sporty for a person with big problems about the water, but even in the secure confines of our cockpit, I could always be found tightly strapped into a life vest, with white knuckles grasping the coaming.

The marina was a two-hour drive from our apartment, and we soon got into the habit of spending the weekends there on the new boat, sailing a bit and just generally soaking up the nautical atmosphere, because chicken that I was, I still enjoyed acting like a sailor. As time went on we realized that since most of our city-based entertaining and being entertained took place on the weekends—when we were too far away to return solely for the evening's agenda—we were gradually phasing out of many of our social relationships and were locking into a new group of people who spent their weekends sailing. In retrospect we realize that the major bonus of breaking patterns and adopting new ones has been the people factor. Our good friendships didn't suffer from our switch of interests, since we were careful to keep those going during the week; however, the superficial associations slipped away and everyone, on both sides, must have been the better for it. In the meantime we were spending a lot of time with people who shared with us a strong common interest.

The Pattern Breakers who fascinated us most in our newly acquired nautical life were the various live-aboarders who were either passing through our area or were based there for a time. At first it was hard to understand why anyone would want to live in the cramped quarters of a boat, but there was an air about these folks that drew us to them. Regardless of age they appeared to be consummately fit, physically and mentally, and on our way back to the city from the docks, Tom and I would spend the full two hours rehashing the time we had shared with these unconventional people. The same subject was constantly cropping up the following week. On most weekends we could be found paying long visits to those cozy vessels—shining of varnish and brass and redolent of home-baked bread or other goodies—listening to the owners' adventures and just generally trying to figure out what accounted for their vigor and seemingly endless enthusiasm. But above all, we wanted to know what their real reasons were for adopting such an unusual life-style.

I recall one lady sailor, in her early seventies, who looked remarkably trim in a bikini, her long, blond hair, mixed with gray, caught in a ponytail. The first time we met her, she had dinghied pell-mell up to the dock and dashed over to her husband, who was conversing with us, to inform him that she had just saved their boat from going onto a reef. The anchor had dragged, and with the engine out of commission, she had been lucky enough to attach a line to an old barge as she and her floating home moved past.

"Everything we have is on that boat!" she said to me, and I was not so much impressed by the precariousness of the life she was leading as by the flash of excitement in her eyes . . . the fact that she looked totally alive—involved—at an age when the most exciting thing many women have to do is to bake chocolate chip cookies for the grandchildren.

The vibrancy projected by this plucky septuagenarian reminded me of another person of her general age whom we had known for many years—a man who met every day with not only a willingness but also a yen to change, and who would nearly always greet us with the exclamation, "I'm starting the most fantastic new project!" (which sometimes involved total uprootings, moves hither and yon, thorough revampings of his life-style) . . . of a pair of middle-age cyclists from Australia who were traveling around the world, carrying their folding bikes with their luggage (two soft bags) on the plane, bus, or train . . . of an eighty-year-old man who had left the households of his solicitous offspring to provide a completely self-sufficient life for himself on an isolated mountain in the South . . . of a number of people we had known, young and old, who chose to live on the fine edge of challenge.

As our involvement with the nautical life continued, Tom and I gradually fell into the practice of inviting our live-aboard friends to use our apartment as a base for shopping in the city. Juxtaposed against our secure and predictable environment, our houseguests, though dressed fairly routinely for their excursion to the metropolis, seemed somehow different. They were usually older than we were, since having the funds to live aboard often implies retirement, but their vibes appeared to be more akin to those of our sons and their peers than to ours, and I would feel almost apologetic when showing them their comfortable quarters. Their atypical life-style seemed to call for more down-to-earth surroundings. As I would lead them through the apartment, I would get the distinct feeling that there was more to life than hot showers and ample kitchens and that Tom and I had literally and figuratively missed the boat. Furthermore, our guests were always much more impressed by the sharpness of our knives and by the heavy-duty stainless used in our pots and pans than by our giant-size refrigerator and central air-conditioning. Books and good music seemed to be high on their list of priorities. And it was not unusual for a couple to spend their time curled up with a good book or listening to records, and to go back to the docks with no errands done and no regrets whatsoever.

Only in small children and teenagers had we seen such flexibility and freedom. Indeed, the overall impression we had of our live-aboard friends was that their challenging mode had set their real ages back decades. Although most of them had raised families and had at one time had life-styles resembling our own, the day-to-day testing of all their faculties aboard a small sailing vessel had made them different . . . had made them younger and healthier. Swiftly and surely Tom and I began to change our minds about what we wanted out of life. We decided to break the continuum that was leading us irrevocably in the direction of old age and ill health. I would overcome the remaining traces of fear, we would find the proper boat, and we would break free as soon as our finances permitted.

The type of route we chose—the drastic geographical change, the move to a totally different life-style, the complete uprooting, cleaning out, and starting all over again—is probably the surest way to attain a life full of challenge, and hence of youth and health. However, there are many innovators who have been unable to make geographical breakaways because of family responsibilities or other reasons, or who simply haven't wanted to move away, and who have still succeeded in injecting constant challenge into their lives.

A good example of people who stay at home and at the same time are adventurers can be found in ham radio operators. Since ham radio is one of our hobbies, Tom and I have had the good fortune of becoming deeply involved with many of the members of this network of people, the majority of whom are based on land. Serious ham operators throughout the world have more than their hobby in common. They have the gleam in their eyes of true Pattern Breakers, since they are, after all, traveling all over the globe every day. Participants in this varied life-style often work at regular jobs or are Recommencers; in actuality, however, many of those who are still working are managing to attend to the airwaves a large part of the time, chatting with hams from their region via handsets when in vehicles, on coffee breaks, or at the lunch hour, and communicating from more complicated home-based rigs with their peers in Russia, Japan, or on some isolated atoll in the Pacific. A university professor we know spends his vacations visiting hams he has met on the air, often in faraway places, and his house is a virtual United Nations as foreign operators come and go. The ham radio scene is full of many types of challenges. Long hours are often spent in rescue efforts; the technical aspects of hooking up with satellites, or simply of establishing contact with distant spots by any means, keep these energetic men and women on their toes, and regular contests—some of a quite grueling nature—refine all the necessary skills.

Another group of people who see the world from the vantage point of the Old Hometown are those generous individuals who open their arms and hearths to foreign students—young guests who are eager to share their cultures with anyone who is interested. This and other methods of reaching out to countries abroad always guarantee excitement. But as many successful Pattern Breakers know, the adventuresome approach to life does not have to be oriented to constant contact with other countries. For example, opening an innovative kind of business or giving full rein to those long-suppressed creative urges can revolutionize the whole spectrum of attitudes, habits, and activities and can bring a totally different set of friends and acquaintances onto the scene. Any route that keeps people in familiar surroundings—whether their contacts are with points near or far—bears the danger of all those old negative patterns that are still lurking about. But Pattern

Breakers who keep an alert eye out for the traps can find just as many rewards at home as their gypsy counterparts find abroad.

For those who decide to make the big break with old patterns and take up an entirely new life-style, in any location, the best way to test how different the new mode is from the old way of life would probably be to ask, how easy is it? If everything just glides along, if there are too few times when you have to wrack your brain and put all your emotional and physical resources on the line, beware; most likely, too many threads of the old patterns are still holding strong. Ease appears to equate with security and sameness, not with challenge and zestful living.

This is not to say that the only way to have fun is to systematically deprive oneself; rather, the message is that adventure is enjoyment and that we can either go through our three score and ten and hopefully many more in a somnolent state or we can wake up and commence an unconditional experience with life.

Back in our secure and too-comfortable days, our senses were far less perceptive. After all, we lived in a largely insulated environment. Even the vagaries of the weather had scant influence on us, our sole effort in that regard generally being to turn on the windshield wipers or close the windows. Seen from the safety of our home, a storm would bend the trees and flood the streets, but our protected setting made the affair quite unimportant. On Romany Star we scan the skies for the hint of a storm; if we're sailing, we may get wet and chilled, and we may feel a bit apprehensive as we go through the heightened wind and waves. Later we change our clothes and have the cozy feeling of getting warm and dry again. This constant stimulation of the senses makes life infinitely finer in all respects. After a tangle with the forces of nature, all the good things are better—a tasty meal, a sound night's sleep, a gorgeous view, a sexual happening.

On the other hand, since we aren't masochists, a major victory is a rest from problems of any kind—perfect weather, perfect anchorage, no mechanical hassles. But it's the challenging experience that we cling to . . . such as the night when a storm caught us in the infamous Anegada Passage with all sails up, and we were able to come through without a hitch . . . or the day we found ourselves without wind or functioning motor and succeeded in paddling our fairly large boat off a reef with dinghy oars. This varying mixture of the hard with the easy provides no time or reason for growing old and tired.

The complex role of challenge in zestful living was perfectly illustrated by some friends we recently visited on the picturesque little island of St. Bart's. After a two-day sail from the U.S. Virgin Islands, we slipped into the peaceful harbor of Gustavia shortly before lunch, with several hours to eat, clean up the boat, and then rest a bit before getting ready for dinner with this interesting pair, residents of St. Bart's for the past twenty years. Marge, a writer and illustrator of children's storybooks, and Don, a retired musician, had visited us a number of times in the States, when they were back on shopping excursions. Although we had received many invitations to visit them, this was the first time we had been able to make the trip. We were eager not only to see our friends but also to inspect the unusual house they had built—doing much of the labor themselves—on a rocky hill overlooking the northwest coast of the island.

At sunset we dinghied to the main wharf, occupied by a large, modern cargo vessel from France. Pulling ourselves up and onto the high, concrete dock, we fell, literally, into the arms of our waiting hosts. The excited chatter didn't flag all the way to their home—first through the quaint town, with its colorful old buildings, bearing signs printed in French, and then up a narrow, paved road that took incredibly sharp turns. Our emotions still at high pitch, we toured the estate they had developed during the past two decades. It was an impressive, sprawling stone house—far grander than anything we had expected—with gardens of bright flowers and laden fruit trees extending down to a private dock at the edge of the bay. The rear of the house opened up, through banks of shutter-type doors, onto a long stone terrace, which offered a stunning panorama of islets, cays, jutting rocks, and, across a wide expanse of water, the lofty hills of St. Martin.

Over dinner Tom summed up what we had been exclaiming in

bits and pieces ever since our arrival: "You two have done an unbelievable job here!"

"Want to buy it?" Don asked.

Marge added, "We're anxious to get away!"

The excitement of our arrival had toned down by now, and for the first time I noticed that our friends had definitely lost their old sparkle. Our memories of them had been of two superenthusiastic people always bursting with vim and vigor; in fact, no one had been very surprised back in the days when they first came up with the odd idea of building a house on a tiny little island far from home. "That's Marge and Don for you!" was the admiring reaction; we had all begun to adventure vicariously through them. On their trips back they had been indefatigable—rushing from party to party, brimming over with stories of their struggles on an island that was quite primitive at the time. Now they looked old and tired. They must be ill, I worried.

"This place is too civilized now," Don sighed. "Everything's too easy—supermarkets . . . restaurants . . . people . . . too many people."

"It was a lot more fun," Marge interposed, "when we had only the little shops and what the native boats brought into the dock."

"Nothing but a horse or jeep could make it to our place," Don chortled. "Most of the materials for this house were carried up on horseback or in wagons. What a ball!" He settled back, smiling with the memory.

"There are people all over the place now," Marge said. "They're building closer and closer."

I had never known these two to eschew the company of others; furthermore, on our trip up we had seen only two houses within a half mile of their grounds.

"Where do you plan to go?" I was afraid of the obvious answer.

"To Florida . . ." Marge confirmed my fears, "to be near good hospitals and doctors."

"Is there something wrong?" Tom's face showed concern over this terrible thing that was happening to our old friends.

"Not really," Marge said, "but at our age . . ."

Later, as they drove us back to the dock, they recounted uproarious tales of mind-boggling hassles they had experienced during the years when they were building their house: how they had routinely been forced to fly to nearby St. Martin, in small planes with marginal safety features, in order to secure many of the basic necessities of life; how they had often had to turn to the generous local people—most of them descendants of the Norman French—for assistance in coping with this or that problem.

Before starting our trip back down to Gustavia, we had invited Don and Marge to come out to the boat for an after-dinner drink, and they had refused. "Too late, and we're a bit tired," Don had said. But arriving at the bay on the wave of one of their hilarious stories about old-time St. Bart's, we coaxed them into the dinghy—a physical feat they accomplished with the agility of persons half their age.

Shortly before dawn—after another long session of tales about the good old days—we took them ashore, the four of us laughing and singing all the way, and watched as they nimbly negotiated the upward distance from dinghy to cement. From an all-fours position they sprang to their feet, waved, and threw kisses and whisked into their car.

As we motored out toward Romany Star, Tom switched to neutral for a while and allowed us to drift in the light of the full moon, letting the stillness seep into what had been a decidedly hyper night.

After a few moments of quiet I asked, "Well, what's your opinion? Should they move to Florida?" As we looked back, we could see the bright sweep of our friends' headlights cutting a wedge from the dark hilltop behind Gustavia.

"I may be wrong," Tom said slowly, in a tone that implied that he knew he was right, "but I think that Marge and Don shouldn't waste any time finding themselves another backward island . . . and the sooner they start hassling to build a big, complicated house on it, the better!"

N E W
L I F E - S T Y L E S

Come see what I brought!" Tom sang out as he slammed the front door shut behind him. "A Retirement Package . . . let's check it out!"

Since the usual repository of big items—the dining table—had already been shipped off to relatives to await the day when one of our sons might want it, the best place to open up the big cardboard box was on the living room rug. I could hardly wait to see the contents of this unanticipated link to our new life. At this point, with our recommencement only a few days away, we were living on an unflagging emotional high, and every event had become a cause for celebration. I found myself wondering, though, how these important mystery items would fit into Romany Star's crowded lockers.

"I didn't know there *was* such a thing as a Retirement Package," Tom said as he struggled happily with the stapled box top, "till I went to personnel today to sign a bunch of pension papers. Richards said the box just arrived from the central office, and he didn't know what was in it, either." He finally succeeded in ripping off the cardboard top, exposing, to our palpable disappointment, a boring-looking stack of pamphlets and folders.

"More pension stuff to wade through!" I tried not to sound too deflated as I plucked the top-offering from the pile and began reading aloud, with Tom peering over my shoulder, " 'Things to

Do in Your Mature Years.'" Thumbing through it I continued, "'Stamp Collecting'" (illustration of genial-looking old-timer wearing cable-knit cardigan, sitting at table and peering through pair of spectacles at open stamp-collector's album); "'Coin Collecting'" (illustration much the same except for old fellow's face and color of sweater); "'How to Raise Vegetables in Your Own Backyard'" (our contented friend—slightly different face and minus sweater—now leaning on hoe next to three neat rows of what appeared to be lettuce, tomatoes, and carrots); "'Let's Go Fishing'" (couple in small motorboat on rippleless lake, holding fishing rods and displaying serene smiles—if they sank, would they go down smiling?).

Tom's eyes met mine as I looked up. I rushed to the company's defense, "Well, there's nothing wrong with any of this. In fact you've always been interested in coins . . . you want to raise food someday, and you like to fish."

"Yeah," he said, in a decidedly let-down tone, "but the way they've put it all together—it's so . . . so sedentary!

"Let's check out this folder." As he pried the shiny gray packet open, a number of slick printed sheets tumbled out: "Investing for Security," "Making the Most of Your Lifetime Savings," "How to Keep Your Savings Safe."

"Everything is so safe! How about a little healthy risk?" I grumbled. "And what do we have here?" I flicked dispiritedly at another ministack of folders: "Health Tips for Your Retirement Years," "Exercises to Keep Fit" (with picture of elderly woman lying on floral-patterned rug while lifting one leg a few inches in the air), "The Five Most Common Ailments after Age 60," "Does Your Health Insurance Fill the Bill?," "Disease Prevention in the Mature Years."

Tom summed up the last one: "Morbid . . . this is all too morbid. I don't want to start specializing in diseases!" Too sedentary, too safe, too morbid—we were beginning to sound like Goldilocks.

Somebody had to be wrong—either this solemn pair of would-be adventurers, sitting in yoga position in the living room of their

23

already-sold residence, looking at each other over a pile of unwanted booklets and papers, or the people who were beaming the depressing message that after retirement it's downhill all the way. For a moment neither of us spoke. Then, in a swoop, each gathered up an armload and headed with quiet determination for the door. Not till we reached the smoke-scented confines of the incinerator room did we break down into laughter. By the time the clump of printed matter had slid down the chute and into the furnace's innards, we were doubled over. Back in our apartment, sipping a self-congratulatory glass of wine, we agreed that burning that pompous array of negative vibes was one of the most cathartic acts of our entire lives.

Before making our big move into a new life-style, we had covered ourselves adequately—healthwise with good insurance, financially with enough to live in reasonable comfort on land or sea, and activitywise with plans that should keep us full of zip for years to come. Most important, though, we had adamantly turned down those stereotyped passive roles that choke all the initiative out of so many retirees; our plans, as Recommencers, were ambitious enough to satisfy a teenager. At the time of life when a slowdown is not only expected but usually programmed, we were going to have to employ every bit of intelligence and energy we had to make a success of our new pattern. We certainly did not lack in desire.

Genuine desire may very well be the Number One requisite for establishing new patterns. Wanting to change can be a miraculous "enabler," even compensating, in many cases, for missing qualities and abilities. Of course the transition is much smoother for those who carry into their new lives not only a genuine desire to change but also generous stores of interests, experience of all kinds, and talents. Whereas material possessions from the old life tend to weigh us down and hinder our flexibility, personal qualities and abilities are the threads we use in weaving the new tapestry.

When contemplating a giant step out of one pattern and into another, one should study every facet of the new mode through the window of his or her individual grounding and personality traits, at the same time leaving lots of room for future growth and change. At first glance, the move into a live-aboard life would appear preposterous for the two principals here—myself, a former English teacher, of late an executive's wife who did some writing on the side and who had a wretched history of water-related fear, and my husband, a man whose successes had mainly been in the cosmopolitan arena of buying and selling. How could these two even consider a life suspended on a mere chip of fiberglass floating on the ocean—a life of struggles that, above all, entailed mechanical and commonsense aptitudes?

But the facts were these: Tom had always longed to know more about mechanics, carpentry, and electronics; I enjoyed writing but found too little material that interested me in my old routine. We shared a passion for travel and a desire to know all kinds of people from every walk of life. Also, we liked organization and efficiency, and the boat—where every item must have a purpose—indulged this inclination. We enjoyed studying, and the need to acquire navigation skills and other sea-related information provided material for a lifetime.

A key element in our success as live-aboards can be found in the dynamics of our personal relationship. A lot of married people are deeply in love but simply cannot tolerate a twenty-four-hour, everyday exposure to each other. Owing to our interests, some shared, some quite individual, we can be content living in close quarters. "Doing our own thing," such as writing and studying, provides the emotional space we need. Judging by the live-aboards we have known, the success of the venture may very well revolve around this fragile pivot; we have seen many sincere efforts fail because the constant contact has proved damaging to the relationship. Any new pattern, on land or sea, that involves limited space and continual closeness of two or more people should be carefully evaluated beforehand. There are many ways to alleviate the problem—an area, even a tiny one, which is off-limits to all but the occupant . . . a mutual respect for privacy, for times to just sit and think . . . buffers such as curtains and partitions. The approach that is doomed for failure is the one that pretends the problem doesn't exist.

After the emotional facets of the new life-style have been honestly assessed (for example, how much can you sacrifice and still be sure that your pleasure quotient is satisfied?), the Pattern Breaker's interests and abilities will open the way into rewarding situations. In fact interests from the old life can develop in astounding ways when given a new setting. And since not everyone can afford, or desires, to quit earning money, new patterns can offer lucrative rewards, too. Since our recommencement Tom and I have both developed activities that produce occasional cash. After working for three decades with a large retail concern, he finds it interesting to do consulting work for marine stores from time to time, and since our new life has brought a wealth of material for writing, I enjoy doing articles for the various sail magazines. Needless to say, I'm also into book writing.

One enterprising couple known to us loved to travel, but as owners of a small furniture store, had little money for it. In their late fifties they turned their lives squarely around by selling out their stock and becoming representatives of various furniture lines, this new venture providing them with constant travel to other countries. Their personalities have flourished in the new ambience. No longer do they project the aging "mom and pop" image; instead they have metamorphosed into world travelers, with accompanying changes in their dress and in the topics of conversation they are eager and well equipped to discuss. Having always lived in a conservative house in the suburbs of Miami, they have now graduated to a glamorous condominium overlooking Biscayne Bay.

Another pair—she a legal secretary with a penchant and ability for cooking, he an unenthusiastic motel manager who would go to almost any length to play hooky and go swimming at the beach—left the city life to run a private and very posh club-resort on a small island in the Caribbean. Since business is seasonal, they have several long, sleepy months each year when work tapers off and they can give their full attention to having fun.

26

One of the most memorable Pattern Breakers we've met owned a small restaurant but virtually lived for the one day a week when his business was closed and he could go flying in a rented plane. After a couple of years he sold out *in toto*, bought a small plane, and started transporting lobsters from the Florida Keys to points north. We made his acquaintance at a small airport in North Florida, where he was off-loading his cargo. After hearing his unusual story, we stood outside the small office building and watched as he hopped into his plane and winged off against the blue sky. The impression was that of a perfectly happy man.

In contrast to the case of the happy pilot, for other Pattern Breakers the restaurant business can be the fulfillment of dreams. In the early years of our marriage we had a very good friend, older than we were, who liked nothing better than jamming his backyard to capacity with hungry guests, then proceeding to ply them with lovingly tended, mouth-watering barbeque. He was with the same retail outfit as my husband, and though he was quite successful as a merchandiser, his heart was in feeding people. He broke a lot of patterns when he decided to leave his white-collar job and open a small barbeque restaurant in a distant city. Over the years his business has developed into a nationwide franchise, but it is not unusual to see our friend at the original restaurant, near his home, dashing in and out of the kitchen, greeting customers, and still enjoying the food atmosphere. The fact that he no longer needs the money is irrelevant to him.

Knowledge of a foreign language can give a real advantage to the Pattern Breaker. A middle-age woman we know, bored with teaching high school French, secured a job as instructor in an English academy in Paris and later traveled to French Guiana to do translating for an American business there. Teachers of almost any subject can generally find employment as English professors in foreign countries if they know even the smallest amount of the native language. On the other hand, in areas such as Saudi Arabia—where American aviation companies have large facilities—and on U.S. military bases worldwide, knowledge of a foreign language isn't a requisite. The advantages of teaching overseas were well illustrated by a couple we met while Romany Star lay at anchor in Isles des Saintes, south of Guadeloupe. This adventuresome pair were cruising on a boat they had chartered, and over evening drinks in our cockpit, informed us that they were employed in Saudi Arabia—he in the office of an aviation company and she as a fourth-grade teacher for English-speaking children whose parents worked for the company. They received a paid round-trip fare back to the States each year and had found, to their elation, that owing to airline ticketing practices, they could fly around the globe almost as cheaply as flying direct from their job site to their hometown. Not only were they seeing the world, but also they were living well, and since many of their overseas living expenses were paid for, they were saving a good deal of money.

Language is no barrier in the Bahamas, of course, and a fellow we met on a trip there was living a singular example of turning experience and talents to good use in breaking patterns. He had closed his small machine shop in the Midwest and had opened one in the unorthodox setting of his tiny house, located in a shady grove above a sparkling bay. A couple of hefty machines dominated his living room, and he was busy as a bee, fixing and fashioning a variety of parts for engine installations. Since there was no road up to his place, his clients had to struggle up a rocky path to reach him, and he always had something cool for them to drink at the end of their arduous climb. He was well known for his mechanical abilities, but his working uniform was perhaps the most memorable—a bikini that just barely served its purpose.

A deep desire to do a specific thing is often indication enough that the talents to be successful are present. A national publication recently carried the story of an ad agency executive who left the big city, relocated, and became a well-paid harbormaster—a job apparently totally unrelated to his training, but, in truth, perfectly suited to his abilities. People are complex creatures, and many talents lie undiscovered in all of us—a fact that makes pattern breaking not only rejuvenating but just plain common sense. We can never tell when a change will reveal amazing things about ourselves.

One of the most surprising recommencements we have witnessed has been that of a man who was once owner of a successful auto equipment store. His pattern-breaking experiences have been as astonishing to himself as to those around him. If anything, before leaving the business world, he was apolitical, casting his vote in elections without making more than a cursory inspection of the candidates, and certainly never lending a hand to anyone's campaign. With more time on his hands, however, he began reading about the issues and consequently became concerned about the kind of people who were running the local government. He ran for a city commissioner post—to his amazement, won, and became a powerful force for change in his city. He then moved on to the state capital. From store owner to the state legislature seems like a big leap, but close scrutiny of his career would show that he had been dealing every day with the wants and needs of people—handling complaints, working out solutions of all kinds to satisfy the customer, achieving the maximum output from his employees, managing money.

Farming attracts a lot of people who have spent their lives in the city. Tom and I are fascinated by the idea of growing our own food on a small farm and someday will have that experience; self-sufficiency plays a large role in our boating life, and we would try to organize the farm setup in accordance with that concept. Farming ventures can become big business, also, and two Recommencers we know who started commercial projects on their farms are now in the big-time: one raises turkeys in the hills of North Carolina, and the other has pecan groves in Georgia.

Foreign countries where the dollar enjoys a good position sometimes offer a cost of living so low that living there is a money-maker in itself. A sixtyish couple we met on a trip back to the States confided that they were selling their home and buying a small house in the Dominican Republic, where they could virtually live "like kings" on less than a thousand dollars a month. Recommencers are also moving to Spain and other European countries, where they rent or buy living quarters and use their new location as a takeoff spot for excursions into a multitude of contrasting cultures. Others are touring Europe by recreational vehicle or van. Amsterdam is one of the favored places for purchasing this kind of live-in transportation at a reasonable price, with the dealers buying back at a discount when the trip is over. Guadalajara, Mexico, has long been a drawing card for both wealthy and money-conscious Recommencers from the United States. Generally speaking, however, areas that aren't heavily influenced by tourists are the least expensive; in tourist spots, even though the dollar is worth much more than the local currency, merchants have a way of jacking prices up and erasing the benefits for the American spender.

Along the general lines of the above is the life-style, referred to in a previous chapter, that Tom and I plan to incorporate with our sailing pattern: spending several months a year in small-town settings in various countries abroad. Leaving Romany Star securely propped up on chocks, we will take off, and when the chill winds descend, fly back to the Caribbean, have our floating home lowered back into the water, and sail away to near or distant spots. The economics of this plan are sensible, since air fare and other relocating expenses will be more than equaled by cost-of-living savings. (Prices are high in many of the areas to which we enjoy sailing.) Recommencers with the most modest of fixed incomes have mind-boggling opportunities for seeing the world in the way that we are projecting. Though a preliminary inspection trip to the target country is the smartest way to go, a lot of good information can be obtained through tourism bureaus. Renewable residency can usually be achieved through passport submission, financial data showing solvency, a police certificate from one's last town of residence, results of a health exam, and a list of immunizations. A wealth of new patterns—new languages, cultures, different people—are at one's fingertips in this country-to-country experience.

There is no set way for breaking patterns; it is a very personal venture, and the people involved are the only authorities as to which direction to take or how far to go. Just as when starting an exercise program, an individual who is acquiring a new life-style must start right where he or she is. In other words what is a tiny step for one person can be a giant step for another. The Pattern Breaker must be prepared to completely ignore the lavish and sometimes well-meaning opinions of relatives and friends, since this input is usually so negative that it will slow down, if not totally destroy, all those exciting plans. One of the happiest and most moneywise couples we have ever met had braved the objections of their distressed offspring and sold everything upon leaving the business world. They proceeded to put a sizable piece of cash into the purchase of a very comfortable thirty-foot RV. First of all they made a yearlong tour of the United States, noting carefully the places they particularly liked; the second year they began their return to those favorite spots, and are staying as long as they wish in each place. Longer jaunts—to Canada, Alaska, and Mexico— are on their future agenda. The high cost of gasoline is now outweighed by the fact that they stay put for longer periods. They buy a used car at each new location and sell it when they leave; since one of the husband's hobbies is mechanics, he improves each car and usually makes a profit on the resale. The wife had learned calligraphy before retirement and finds as much work as she wants, doing the lettering on documents and award certificates, for favorite verses and sayings . . . whatever her clients desire. In the process she meets a lot of people and learns about the community.

We were visiting recently with these travelers' son and his mate, and, as always, the evening's conversation turned around the mobile pair. We asked about the other set of in-laws, who resided nearby, and with a hurried "They're fine . . . we talk to them on the phone or see them every day," that subject was disposed of, and the two were chattering animatedly again about the see-America adventurers. The younger couple had laid plans for joining the big tour at different points, whenever they could get vacation time from their jobs. Mom and Dad had clearly proved their point.

Adventures in building houses can bring challenge to the Pattern Breaker's life, and if the location is an unusual one, or if the house incorporates innovative features, the adventure will continue long past the building stage. For a number of years we have enjoyed a relationship with a couple who left the world of formal employment in their fifties to erect a modest home on an island that is almost squarely in the center of a large northern lake. There was only one other resident on the island—an old-timer who fished and trapped for a living. Our friends had opted for a year-round experience, which involved not only dealing with isolation from the mainland during heavy snows but also with facing difficulties at many times of the year in crossing the lake by motorboat to reach the nearest grocery store. Though enjoying the unpolluted peace of their surroundings, these enterprising people were not hermits by nature and often had someone visiting. Guests—and there was a waiting list of friends wanting to share in the adventure—helped clear the snow and do other chores. Recently a developer started a summer resort complex on the island, and the now-septuagenarian couple have decided to try metropolitan life again. They're still doing things a bit differently, though; they're building a comfortable log-cabin home on the outskirts of Minneapolis.

A fiftyish couple we met on a trip to Ohio—they had been involved in house construction there—had decided to collect their winnings and use their abilities to build a purely self-sufficient home adjacent to a river. They had produced stacks of plans for the cooling and heating systems and for water purification, wind generator for power, gardening plots, food preservation systems such as drying, canning, freezing. A life full of challenge lay ahead of this energetic duo.

Another couple purchased a small warehouse and five acres of land on the outskirts of their town, then proceeded to turn the building into an attractive and comfortable residence—a project that lasted for several years. His business experience in the field of heavy machinery has left him with an affinity for mechanical apparatus in general, and with the help of a variety of small machines, they have turned their land into a beautiful and productive area, with flowers and a wide range of vegetables and fruit trees.

Since pattern breaking starts from the precise point where the Pattern Breaker is standing, a relatively simple move to an entirely different city, or within the same city, can be a real adventure for some people. Daily life in a new setting can be quite challenging for a person who has lived all or most of his or her days in the same place. We met a full-of-pep pair of Recommencers in Knoxville, Tennessee, who had moved there from Akron, Ohio, birthplace for both of them. It was clear that these two felt as adventuresome as any pioneer who had ever wagon-trained through the Old West. Finding their way around and making new friends had filled them with zest for living.

Some of the most challenging adventures are taking place right in the midst of the old, familiar setting, and the Pattern Breakers involved are enjoying a full measure of rejuvenating benefits. Success in establishing new patterns in old settings can usually be accurately gauged by the frequency and number of new faces that become a part of the Pattern Breaker's world. In the final analysis, as we find in our lives on a sailboat and observe from the lives of other adventurers we meet on land and sea, the real gold for Pattern Breakers is in the people they meet.

An all-involving pattern as a full-time student can change one's life completely, providing a totally new set of "tracks," new friends, and new habits. The same kind of results can be obtained from serious involvement in a health food and exercise regimen. Interest in health food provides study that never ends, along with a lot of new relationships and a vastly different shopping routine. Exercise can include calisthenics and aerobics classes, plus the full spate of athletics available in one's area. And all the while, these stay-at-homes have the good fortune of being able to maintain close contact with those deep, important relationships that have been honed and tested through the years.

Ham radio, included in chapter two, is an excellent new pattern in an old setting. A lot of challenge is involved in obtaining the novice license, and challenge continues to be a part of this life-style as higher-grade certificates are acquired, as technical advances and financial capability enable the individual to build more and more potential into his or her rig, and as contests are staged (for example, one in which an award is given for the person who can contact the largest number of foreign-based hams or make the most satellite-relayed contacts in a given period of time).

Everyone has some kind of creative bent, and total immersion in a life mode built on these kinds of talents can be supremely rewarding. Since creativity can take place, literally, on the head of a pin, as in sewing, travel is not a requisite. Halfway involvement in the artistic life results in nothing more than a hobby, without the renewing benefits that are experienced in a full-fledged break with old patterns and entrance into a new way of life. I recall a man in his sixties who had been a policeman but—rugged appearance and thick hands aside—had always wanted to paint. He took lessons in painting on ceramics and acquired an entirely different life-style while working at his craft, exhibiting, and, as a great extra benefit, selling. A musician friend found that guitar lessons were excellent therapy for emotionally disturbed young people and established a rewarding new pattern for himself and his students.

Collectors' hobbies are excellent subpatterns that can be enjoyed without leaving town, but unless the collector branches out into total involvement—extensive travel to conventions and other hobbyist gatherings, along with all-out service to the hobby's organizations—this type of activity will usually not be strong enough to effect a break with the old continuum. Shelling, searching for scrimshaw, and other kinds of collecting that call for a lot of moving about sometimes provide the framework for genuine pattern breaking.

Business ventures can be taken up at any age and can be great pattern breakers, as well as income producers, in the heart of the old environment. Many people have in mind a business they would like to own, but too often these would-be adventurers haven't been able to muster the nerve to make the first move. Of course it isn't good sense to put all one's life savings on the line, but if the money angle can be sensibly managed, the experience can be invigorating. A number of Recommencers purchase motels and find the money good and the exposure to travelers stimulating. Handyman businesses, which cost little to set up, are going extremely well these days, with men and women doing such jobs as installing doors, drapes, washers and dryers; repairing cabinetry; painting houses. Meeting new people is an important part of this kind of undertaking. A businessman who became a Pattern Breaker in his hometown had played the piano for his own pleasure since childhood and had wanted for years to become a piano tuner. As a Recommencer he paid for classes, purchased the tools, and now has more requests than he can cover. He confesses that he has never been happier. "When I get a piano perfectly tuned," he says, "it's almost as if I'd saved a life!"

Some of the bravest and most interesting Pattern Breakers are those who, right in the midst of people they have known for years, take a stand that diametrically opposes common belief or practices. Examples are those who espouse unpopular causes; the small business owner who hires only ex-convicts; the motel owner who accepts only nonsmokers; business people who put their finances on the line for all kinds of methods that go against usual practices; the kind souls (and many have been reported across our nation) who don't depend on the welfare system to feed the hungry, but instead launch food-for-the-poor campaigns of their own; people who seek friends from all levels of life, refusing to associate solely with those who are "socially acceptable"; teachers who risk dismissal by following their deepest convictions about the education process; nurses who put their jobs on the line by standing firm for what is good for the patient.

One of the most amazing people I have met is smashing patterns every day, right and left, in the town where she has lived for thirty years. As a member of a black community in Alabama—where there are very strict standards as to what women are supposed and not supposed to do—this brave widow, age sixty-three, is engaged in enough activity to exhaust an athlete. Upon her husband's death five years ago she went back to work as an adoptions officer in the welfare department but in addition to that job has done remarkably well financially by buying and selling bits and pieces of land, and in her spare time, making and selling decorative throw pillows. She is a leader in an awesome number of church, civic, and purely social activities. No small size this lady, but undaunted she travels from one involvement to another mounted on her Honda—*avec* helmet—and is not intimidated by trips covering hundreds of miles. When she went over her first mountain, she told me, she realized that she could do the same in the Rockies. That jaunt is on her agenda.

I met this Superpattern Breaker, who makes everyone around her seem dead by comparison, walking down the dock, looking at sailboats with the fixed plan of buying one to live on when she recommences. She has had very little boating experience, but her success as a live-aboarder is a sure thing.

Sarah and Jim are two of the most innovative Pattern Breakers I have ever known, yet they pulled their feat off right in the city where they had lived for most of their lives. The majority of people who knew them as they used to be feel they "went bananas"; a few close friends admire them. Above all, however, the extent to which they went in seeking a new life-style tells us something about how difficult it can be to change patterns in an old setting, without the benefit of a geographical move.

To give you a clue as to the extent of Sarah and Jim's Big Change, when we first met them, they were Diane and Paul. They had lived a purely ordinary life: he had been quite successful as an investment broker, and she had enjoyed her career as an elementary school teacher. They had three children, who at the time of their parents' revolution were through college and on their own, and to the parents' credit, the breakaway did not violate any of the important ties with their offspring.

I believe it all started when the last child left the nest for his own pad, and they discovered that life had become exceedingly dull. They started taking some evening classes at the nearby university and almost immediately became involved with a younger group who were health food and yoga enthusiasts. On a visit to one of our sons in their city, we were included in a dinner invitation to their home, where we enjoyed a delicious buffet of miso and sea vegetable soup, tofu sandwiches, salads, nuts, and fruits. During a tour of their house, which had been sold and was to be vacated in one week, we were shown a master bedroom that in lieu of a bed displayed a king-size futon, an Oriental type of pad rolled out on the floor. My memory of the evening is dominated by the unusual food, a virtuoso performance on the piano by our host, the futon, a lovely poetry recitation by a college girl, and above all, the glowing faces of Diane and Paul. They were positively rapturous over the new life they were entering.

Their immediate plans were centered around going back to college. He would further his studies in music with the plan of becoming a composer of classical works, and she would study painting, something she had always wanted to do. They would live on campus and would not own a car; they had decided that walking and bicycling were healthy activities, even if they involved rising an hour earlier. Daily yoga and continued adherence to health food would combine with all that rigorous use of their legs to keep them in shape for their exciting futures as composer and painter. As soon as they moved from their house, they would change their names. They felt that such a step would be symbolic of their rebirth.

I must admit that along with their many detractors we thought they were doomed to failure. Everything was just a bit too contrived. Sarah and Jim, however, have had the last word: he is busy composing and has become well known as commentator for a classical music program on a local radio station, and she has just held her first exhibit of paintings—well received, we understand.

For prospective Pattern Breakers who would like to engage in full-time adventuring aboard a boat, the wisest course is to thoroughly try out this unusual life-style before making the final move. A number of factors make this cautious approach the best one: for example, limited space for moving about; the constant motion of the vessel, even when at a marina; conditions that prevail when the boat is under way; many situations of the "House on the Prairie" category, such as getting along with limited water supplies and sometimes having to do the family wash in a bucket. Tom and I were fortunate enough to be able to spend long periods of time on Romany Star before taking our giant step, and for that reason there were few surprises in store for us.

If the Pattern-Breaker-to-be hasn't experienced boating to a significant extent, he or she could help crew with friends before purchasing a vessel. After learning the fundamentals of sailing—or of handling a motorboat, if that is the life-style to be adopted—a small, easily managed craft could be purchased as a first step in ownership. For future Recommencers who have to keep an eagle eye on their money, buying and beginning to outfit the live-aboard boat before leaving the work scene is an excellent idea; costs are more easily absorbed while the bigger paychecks are coming in. A good plan to put into effect before purchasing a boat is to select the area where life aboard will be started and to charter a vessel similar to the one being considered. In this way reactions and needs can be given a fairly good test before the big investment is made. Extensive information on chartering throughout the world can be obtained from the various sail magazines. And these publications are good for a lot of other purposes, such as studying types of boats that are for sale and reading articles about people who are already living on the water.

Despite all the dos and don'ts, however, there is always someone who throws caution to the winds, takes the giant step, and becomes a complete success in the new way of life. Before we made our switch from land to sea, we met two of these impetuous individuals—John and Lou, a middle-age pair who were living on their forty-foot ketch. They had never been on anything bigger than a sailing dinghy, but looking through a sail magazine one day, they decided that they wanted to sell their small pharmacy and take off on a cruising adventure. Purchasing their boat in Miami, they hired a skipper to sail with them to the Caribbean and to teach them everything they needed to know on the way. When we met them, they had been living aboard for two years and in many ways were putting most of their peers to shame. John and Lou enjoyed the feeling of self-sufficiency and had devised a way to keep stores for a year, with the exception of necessary supplies of fresh foods. Constantly sailing to new and different places, they showed no signs of losing their resolve. Since everyone isn't this fortunate, though, it seems prudent to test the sailing life, if possible. If there isn't a choice, adventure must take priority over staying in a rut . . . even if the Pattern Breaker has to back up and start all over again.

There are as many life-styles as there are people. Tom and I are living on the same boat, but for each of us the experience is quite different. Although we both enjoy the lavish display of nature all around us, we are each seeing that beauty through the eyes of our own individual makeup. We both delight in the "feel" of sailing, but at sea Tom will always spend a lot more time concentrating on the trim of the sails, while I find my mind wandering—weaving new stories against the background of water and sky. When Romany Star is at anchor or docked, Tom is busy with the mechanics of the boat, while I—though enjoying lending a hand in repairs—prefer to spend most of our nonsailing time on the appearance of our environment . . . polishing brass, varnishing wood. What matters, however, is that the old personal continuum has been broken for each of us, and the new, invigorating lifestyle, with a good supply and variety of patterns, has gotten under way.

For the prospective Pattern Breaker careful study of a large number of life modes before choosing the right one can be very helpful. But it is well to remember that patterns aren't selected and donned like suits of clothing. Instead the Pattern Breaker will shape the newly adopted mode with his or her own personality, experience, and abilities. And that is precisely what effective pattern-breaking is all about—doing something out of the ordinary, in a different way than it has ever been done before.

MORE COURAGE
FOR BRAVE PEOPLE

f we had listened to the dire warnings of friends and relatives, we would have become quivering masses of flesh. Even the most positive recipients of our big news, that we were going to live and cruise aboard a sailboat, managed to append a gentle message of concern. Actually, it was a surprise that so many people were so concerned about our welfare—even those we had met at that very moment.

The admonitory questions ran the gamut from, What will you do in storms? to, What will you do when you're seventy-five? Our stock answer to the former became, "Oh, there are lots of things to do," and to the latter, "We have no idea . . . What will *you* be doing when *you're* seventy-five?" In the beginning we had often gone to great lengths to give statistics showing how, proportionately, many more people die in cars than in boats, and we had cited cases of octogenarians and even a few nonagenarians who were still sailing across oceans. After a while, however, we got the message: our interrogators were speaking from their own feelings of insecurity . . . from their deep-rooted fear of making changes in their own lives.

Under the guise of security—secure health coverage, secure job, secure home—fear and insecurity have become an integral part of the American way of life. Advances against disease draw top billing in almost any publication, people will sell their souls to keep a job that pays well, and the Family Home—that prototype-forerunner of the mausoleum—offers the final protection to its timorous owners. Underneath all these pretenses, however, lies the certain conviction in everyone's mind that there is far more reason to be afraid than to feel secure.

My own personal victory against fear should give heart to anyone who feels nervous about breaking old patterns and starting a new life. Few people could match my old cowardice, but as the tricks and wiles of my enemy Fear became crystal clear with the passing months, and as I programmed my attack accordingly, I was finally able to rout this crippling force and launch out on a truly fulfilling life. Although my problem was extreme, the same tactics would equally serve the person who feels even the least bit insecure about moving to a foreign country . . . living and traveling in an RV . . . opening a business . . . seeking a self-sufficient style of living on a small farm.

Fear breeds more fear, and until the time I decided to tackle the apprehensions and phobias that were debilitating me, I was becoming more afraid every day. On the other hand, as I began to stand up to my major fear—bit by bit, freeing myself of my water-related phobia—all kinds of seemingly unrelated anxieties began to disappear. Today, with the big battle behind me, I am very careful never to succumb to abnormal fear (some fear is normal), never to back down in a situation that my intellect tells me should not inspire concern. From my own experience I know that every time a person gives in to unreasonable fear of any kind, multiple anxieties are given reinforcement, and the victim becomes more cowardly, physically and emotionally, in many unsuspected ways. For example, the person who decides that airplane travel is too painful and therefore not worth attempting again may find that he or she is beginning to have more problems with claustrophobia (fear of enclosed spaces) or acrophobia (fear of heights) when in elevators; rooftops and high-rise balconies may become untenable.

The fact is that the old enemy Fear has gotten the message. The retreat from flying is laying the path for a retreat from a lot of other activities. That's the bad news. The good news is that the whole thing can be worked in reverse: when one fear is forcefully attacked, the path is laid for increased courage in many other areas.

It is hard to draw a line between physical and emotional fears. Their intertwining and overlapping served me well, however, since through the combined use of physical and emotional tactics, I was finally able to dominate my problems. Hanging onto the ladder of our first cruising boat, the twenty-six-foot sloop—strapped into a life vest and wearing flippers, which alone would not have allowed me to sink—I was, for a long time, unable to release my grasp. Throughout the victories I had achieved up to that point, which included becoming fairly comfortable about sailing, plus managing to get down the ladder and into the water, emotional factors had been a heavy influence. I was enjoying the idea that I was becoming a "real sailor." Lying in bed at home, I would visualize myself sailing solo, swimming and snorkeling like everybody else—allowing myself to feel the emotions of pride, happiness, bravery. On the weekends I would act out, to the extent of my ability at the time, those imagined triumphs, taking small steps toward my goal of being brave. I tried to set up situations that would lead to at least one victory, no matter how minute, to serve as positive reinforcement to my growing valor.

Conscious use of emotions also paved the way to the major breakthrough that finally enabled me to swim away from the boat. Clutching the ladder one day, bulwarked by my everpresent life vest and flippers, in an exquisite bay that combined sparkling water with a background of flower-studded hills and a clear blue sky, I watched with sheer green envy as Tom and our friends disported about a nearby reef. The flash of their bathing suits as they dived and resurfaced, their gleeful cries over a colorful fish they had spotted, added to my unrest. Fully aware of what I was doing, I allowed myself to become a cauldron of envy, self-disgust, and total anger over my exclusion. With dogged determination I swam away from the boat and to the reef. From that day on I never had any difficulty in swimming away from the boat to any point, and soon I was swimming short distances without life vest or flippers.

And as I lost my fear of the water, other fears began to slip away—claustrophobia, which had caused me a great deal of discomfort on elevators (we lived on the fourteenth floor), and a fear of flying that seemed to arise from a number of sources. In addition my growing self-image as a brave person began to make me stronger about facing many types of situations that on the surface were unrelated to physical factors.

Too often people continue in a boring pattern because of a deep insecurity over what would happen if they made a change. Though unhappy with themselves they just can't seem to gather the courage to reach for something better. Emotions—disgust and boredom in relation to the old life, linked with happy anticipation of the new life—consciously wielded, can pave the way to victory. When combined with planned excursions into the new experiences and with programming, insofar as possible, of positive vibes, the uncertainty that is causing the inertia will slip away.

Would-be Pattern Breakers should become familiar with all the tricks that fear can play. "It isn't that I'm afraid; it's just that I don't want to do it" is a reaction that should always be carefully analyzed, since it is an age-old cover-up for qualms. Back in the days when I was terrified of the water, my favorite dodges, which I partially believed, were, "I can't go to the beach because I'm allergic to the sun" (I had once had a skin fungus that had nothing to do with the sun) . . . "The heat is unbearable next to the water" (I completely disregarded the fact that the heat was far from unbearable *in* the water) . . . "I don't want to go to the beach; I want to go shopping" (I had had the whole week for shopping).

Once these tricks are out in the open, a genuine "wanting" for the feared activity can become a powerful emotional weapon for overcoming any apprehensions. When I finally got the real—not imagined—desire to overcome my fear, my struggle was on the way to being won. This desire made me read and learn more about sailing, made me want to feel relaxed and at home in that environment, made me go to great lengths to participate physically in the things that I had previously dreaded.

People who believe that they want to traverse the United States in an RV but who feel insecure about beginning such a gypsy life would do well to read the RV magazines, spend a lot of time in the equipment stores, look at RVs with the idea of purchasing one, spend time in parks where people are camped—getting to know them and talking about their adventures. Renting a vehicle, for a short or longer trip, would be a good idea, too. Soon the genuine desire for that life-style will be so strong that all impediments will fall by the wayside. And after enjoying this vagabond existence for a while, a next step—for instance, living in a foreign country— becomes amazingly easy. When I began to conquer my fear of the water, the last thing in my mind was life aboard a sailboat. As time went by, however, I changed, my desires changed . . . and the live-aboard life became the logical next step.

The man or woman who would like to open a business can gain self-confidence for the venture through use of the emotions, combined with immersion beforehand in the atmosphere of the desired undertaking. It would be wise to form a close relationship with someone who owns a similar establishment, since time spent on the premises under favorable circumstances—soaking up the surroundings, as it were—will do wonders in implanting a positive attitude. The subconscious will get the message that all is well, that only good can come from such a happy change for the better. The genuine wanting will take hold, and at that point the campaign against insecurity will be more than half-won.

Fear is a lamentable cover-up of some of our deepest desires and abilities. When we are enslaved to unreasonable apprehensions, it is difficult to determine from our minds and personalities— choked with all kinds of camouflage—what we really want out of life. Instead we go through our routines mentally and physically circumventing any area that holds the slightest possibility of an encounter with fear. But once this negative emotion is put to flight and the subterfuge-laden victim begins to peel off the pretenses, a whole new world opens up, and a new and different person appears—a person who not only is not afraid to break patterns but who actually welcomes the opportunity.

Prospective Pattern Breakers who are waging campaigns

against fear will find it helpful to set up roadblocks against their own retreat. These uneasy adventurers should tell everyone they know about their plans and should burn the physical bridges behind them by selling or making other arrangements for material possessions that don't fit in. Such acts of determination beam a strong message to the subconscious, where fear has its deepest and darkest caves.

Phobia, or a touch of phobia, often puts an abrupt end to ambitious plans to change patterns. If the new life-style will involve flying, claustrophobia or acrophobia can be an effective dampener. My own major handicap for the sailing life was aquaphobia (fear of water). Some sailors have difficulty with agoraphobia (fear of open spaces), because there's a lot of empty ocean out there! Zoophobia (fear of animals) can limit the adventurer's activities in wooded areas, and theoretically, the list could go on and on, since some people are afraid of the most unexpected things, such as specific numbers (2 or 5, for example). Fear is generally considered to have become phobia at the point where it is totally out of line with the actual danger involved and where it begins to handicap or defeat its victim. From my own experience it is clear that a sincere effort should be made to cast out every kind of abnormal fear. To do otherwise is to limit our lives to a tragic degree, a degree the victim will never completely be aware of unless he or she takes the big step out of that sad condition.

Fear of the unfamiliar crops up in many different disguises. The same culprit that makes people unreasonably wary of foreign governments and foreigners in general will also produce overcaution in making any kind of change in the daily routine. Ventures as simple as taking an adult education course and as complex as moving to a foreign country are hampered by the same old fear of doing anything new . . . anything that isn't completely familiar. Obviously, the best way to attack this enervator is to make, insofar as is possible, the unfamiliar familiar. For example, if future Pattern Breakers have doubts about traveling or living in a foreign country, they should start reading about it, meeting as many of its nationals as possible, learning the language, preparing some of its foods, and before moving—if that's the plan—taking an inspection trip there. Here, as in all Big Changes, the bigger the challenge, the more rejuvenating the experience will be—a truth that should lend comfort to Pattern Breakers who have to try harder than others.

Fears about health entrap many would-be Pattern Breakers, despite the fact that good health is a natural adjunct of a challenging life-style. The medical profession has long acknowledged the influence of the mind on health; studies have even shown that fear of the dreaded disease cancer can be a contributory factor in acquiring it. This knowledge alone should fuel strong efforts to have faith that we will remain well.

There is nothing healthy about rejecting change and, even though one doesn't suffer from any ailment requiring treatment, insisting on remaining near familiar doctors and hospitals. At the same time it makes sense to take advantage of available measures for protecting health, as long as these do not limit our enjoyment of life. A bonus of taking sensible steps is that the whole process helps to erase bothersome fears. We often sail to areas where medical help is of a marginal nature, and for this reason we take adequate stores of medicines, among them, antibiotics, injections for pain, antihistamines for bites and stings. In addition to our health insurance, which is honored in most foreign countries, we carry, when doing long-distance cruising, an insurance that pays the plane transportation of a patient—in horizontal position—from any point in the world (including the United States) to the desired Stateside hospital. Furthermore, we have enrolled in an organization that publishes medical updates on health problems in different countries, along with a list of immunizations needed in various places, and a directory of qualified doctors throughout the world who are members of the organization. (For more data on the insurance and the publications discussed above, see the chapter entitled "Patterns for Good Health.") These are commonsense precautions; however, we believe that our best protector is a refusal to fear illness. In our own experience, and in that of many travelers on land and sea with whom we have regular contact, the health of people who are always on the move is amazingly good. Undoubtedly, the conviction that we must stay well so that we can get the most out of our travels goes a long way in fortifying us. The same would apply to participation in any exciting life-style.

If precautions and reasoning are not enough to quell fears about health in the new way of life, the approaches using the emotions (for example, angrily, How can I be so foolish as to allow fears about my health to ruin my chance for happiness?), visualization of oneself as a healthy participant in a challenging new life, and a sincere wanting to change should do the trick.

Financial fears are another detriment to living a full life. By the same token that health-care safeguards should be set up, it also is wise to establish a firm financial base for your new venture. The key point here might lie in the question, Exactly how much money do I need? Only the person concerned can draw the proper line between what amount is necessary for a happy life and what is actually an excessive calculation prompted by unreasonable fear. When a sensible financial plan has been laid, if apprehensions refuse to fade, the three-pronged attack using emotions, visualization, and sincere wanting—combined, if possible, with time spent with other people who are living the new life-style—should drive away any traces of fear.

People who have always lived near relatives and lifelong friends sometimes fear that moving away will lessen the strength of these emotional ties. Close examination of their foreboding often reveals that the problem is basically one of self-image (I must stay close by to make sure that they'll continue to love me and won't forget me.) Real love, of course, isn't diminished by separation, and persons who do unusual things become quite unforgettable. Trips back home are full of meaning as the adventurer's exploits are discussed and vicariously enjoyed. For Pattern Breakers with children the parenting instincts can go a long way in crushing all fears about separation, for what better example can parents set for their progeny than one of life lived fully at any age? In this way we can be inspiring role models for our children until the day we die. Tom and I find that distance brings us spiritually closer to our loved ones. Correspondence has become extremely important, phone calls are great occasions, and visits—in both directions—are real causes for celebration. Pattern Breakers, living in the ambience of excitement, are always sought out, not only by their chronological age group but also by the younger generation. They usually find that the problem is not one of being left out, but rather one of trying to fit everybody else in.

Fear of failure stymies many a venture into an exciting new pattern. Paradoxically, the fact of failure is one of the best proofs that people should break patterns, since failure at a career or life-style often sets the stage for a new mode with undreamed-of successes. If the individual involved hasn't experienced enough of a failure and has continued to "make it" from day to day, the old unproductive pattern might continue for a lifetime.

The president of a large U.S. corporation declares, "Everyone should have a major career setback at sometime during his or her lifetime." He goes on to say that he failed miserably at his first job and that it was the rude awakening dealt by failure that made him reassess his desires and abilities and head for success. This same kind of effect can be seen in the Cuban immigration of the late fifties and the sixties. Thousands of successful business men and women found themselves penniless in U.S. territory. Though they weren't personally responsible for their plight, the trappings—dingy rooms, a few dollars, only the clothing they could bring in one suitcase—were of utter failure. They began their difficult comeback, usually knowing little English and holding jobs totally unrelated to their former careers, and many have reached a far higher level of success than they would have achieved if they had never suffered a major setback. All of this was accomplished without the advantages they had enjoyed in their native land—perfect command of the language and influential political and business connections.

Fear of failure is usually intertwined with fear of the shame one will feel under the scrutiny of a disapproving public. This is unfortunate, since failure is such a personal matter that the public can never be qualified to distinguish between failure and success.

In the boating life what the public deems success and failure are constantly shown in positions of sharp contrast. The wealthy man's yacht drifts at anchor, almost touching the poor man's small sailboat. The millionaire's tiniest whim is attended to posthaste by a sleekly uniformed crew, and as he dines at an elaborately laid table, he converses frequently by radiotelephone with business interests all over the world. If he elects to forgo business matters while eating, there is still the weight of unattended matters intruding upon his efforts to have a purely social evening. Most likely he'll need his Maalox upon retiring, and his sleep will be fitful as his dreams recap the big financial decisions of the day. On the small sailboat the money-poor owner floats lazily at anchor, eating his catch of the day and enjoying the surrounding display of nature. His sleep is sound—no digestives are needed—and if he dreams, he dreams of fishing and snorkeling and sailing.

Most likely the rich yachtsman and the small-boat skipper feel equally successful. The world, a poor judge, would certainly give short shrift to the latter.

When programming a frontal attack against fear of failure, it is important to set the circumstances for as many successes as possible; in this way the subconscious mind, above all an impressionable element, gets some positive messages: Hey, this person is succeeding at a lot of things! Visualization of ourselves reaching our goal will not only help us to achieve our objectives but will also put a damper on fear of failure. If failure, however, is in the offing, the conscious mind should take this fact as a signpost on the road to success. After all, for those who understand what counts in life, success is a journey, not a destination, and failure is an integral part of that journey, providing the signposts, as it were, for turns in the road. It is interesting to note that brave people are the ones who most often experience so-called failure; the cowardly seldom step out of their secure cocoons long or far enough to do anything but succeed at their trivial efforts.

Although Tom and I never doubted that we would succeed in our new life—perhaps, because we had such a burning desire for it—many of the people around us were far from confident. At every opportunity we were reminded that we might fail. Even today we are encountering surprise on all sides that we are still enjoying the live-aboard life. The reasons for this surprise are the same as those for the admonitory questions we were besieged with when we were starting out on this marvelous adventure: the projection of other people's insecurity upon our own undertakings. If we had failed as live-aboards, however, I'm sure our efforts would not have been wasted. There is no way that we could have landed back in square one; the day we took the giant step from land to sea, we were already entirely different individuals from those two who had lived a mundane, largely homebound existence. For people who are always trying and doing—a good definition of Pattern Breakers—there is no such thing as failure . . . only changes in adventures.

Susie and Frank, some very dear friends of ours, had been planning for several years to make a circumnavigation. Their conversation was always full of eager plans for touching the various ports throughout the world, and a number of their friends became so infected by the couple's enthusiasm that they began long sailing trips of their own—to the Pacific Isles, Europe, South America. Finally, the circumnavigation was set up. The necessary money had been saved, and the boat had been readied with heavy rigging to sustain the mast under ocean gales, a large cockpit dodger to fend off high waves, and a hefty self-steering gear for all those long nights at sea. The takeoff was put into motion, from the British Virgin Islands with the Panama Canal as the first destination. As the sailing vessel hit the massive waves of the deep ocean, both of our friends, having done nothing more than local sailing for a good many years, became violently seasick. After two days and nights of struggling with nausea and fatigue, they made the decision that after all, this really was not what they wanted.

We saw them shortly after their return to the island of Tortola and were glad to find that not a trace of chagrin was present.

"We tried and that's the important thing," Frank said contentedly. "Now we know what we really want—a calm bay to sleep in at night, people around us that we know and like, and a two-hour sail every now and then."

His wife added, with a mischievous grin, "We still may go around the world, though! Who knows?"

FIVE

REJECTING
NEGATIVE VIBES

We had just introduced Ellen and Ralph, who were beginning their recommencement life by putting into effect an energetic new pattern, to thirty-year-old Philip, who had recently returned from a bicycle trip through Europe. The five of us were sitting in a patio cafe on the island of St. Thomas, sipping cool fruit punches, as Ralph, flushed with anticipation of a European tour in a camping van, wrote down Philip's observations on spots of interest that should be included. Whereas the bicycle trip had involved staying in hostels or sleeping in a pup tent, the pair of Recommencers had more money to spend and hence were planning a more comfortable experience— lodging in hotels or inns when suitable campsites, with showers and other benefits, were unavailable.

"We can hardly wait to get going," Ellen exclaimed, "and what good luck to run into someone like you, Philip!"

"Glad to help you," the younger man said, "and I just want you to know that I really admire you two."

Everyone was silent for a moment, till Ralph finally blurted out, puzzled, "*You* admire *us*? Man, *we* aren't seeing Europe on a bicycle with nothing but a backpack for our provisions and clothes!"

"Yeah," Philip said, stretching out his strong, young frame and smiling benignly, "but that's different!"

We were a quartet of boggled witnesses to the Ultimate Age Put-down, which comes thinly disguised as a compliment ("I admire you") but conveys the unmistakable message that the target is some kind of hero simply because he isn't muffled in an afghan, toasting his toes before a fire, sipping from a bottle of iron tonic, and reading the latest issue of his favorite geriatric magazine. When chronologically younger, we were all guilty—without exception—of handing out this kind of hogwash, but that fact is no excuse for the usual attitude of meek acceptance.

One of two ignoble, but quite delicious, routes can be taken on the occasion of an Ultimate Age Put-down. The target can either lapse into a period of obvious stony silence while making a strong inner observation to the effect that the perpetrator is a blatant idiot or can administer a verbal response that will have some mind-altering effects. A lulu of a rejoinder is, "I admire you, too," going on to elaborate at great length why the person, despite the obvious handicap of his youth, is so to be admired. We could call this tactic the Boomerang Parry, since the confusion that has been projected is now back in the ruffled hands of the sender. After this nasty counterattack—which has left your ego in marvelously good shape—be prepared to feel terrible about what you've done and to spend a lot of time being extra nice to your younger opponent.

The third, and purely noble, route is to mentally flush the statement down the toilet and thereby erase its damaging effects from one's memory. Anything is better than meek acceptance, since a submissive attitude delivers a gloomy message to the victim's subconscious to the effect that it's incredible that this individual is doing so much when the sad fact is that at that age a person's too old to be doing anything at all.

To their credit Ellen and Ralph did a great job of the stony-silence route, and Philip had to do some fancy scrambling to bring them back into the conversation. I believe they made their point: they deserved no praise for exercising their right to have fun.

Several years ago I was standing with other family members in the spectators' section beside the finish line of a marathon jogging event, waiting for my nephew to arrive after a grueling ten-mile course. A man about my age had puffed in a few seconds before and was walking in circles, "bringing himself down," as my young kin and another fellow about his age jogged up. After a few moments the three came over, perspiration rolling down their faces, elated that they hadn't done too badly. The families of all three joggers eventually began to converse as our athletes mopped their faces with towels we had brought, and my nephew's friend, a fine young man if there ever was one (the finer they are, the more it hurts), exclaimed to the older competitor, "I really admire you . . . you hung right in there!"

The target of this innocently administered put-down didn't answer, but the look on his flushed and perspiring face said it all: He was an equal competitor with this callow youth—had even come in a few seconds ahead—and he wanted to be admired for his accomplishment and that alone, not for the fact that he did it *at his age*. He didn't want to be a minority (racial minorities endure the same general type of put-down all the time) competing in a marathon; he wanted to be just a bona fide human being competing with other human beings. The implication that he was different had the effect of extracting him from the mass of competitors, setting him to one side, and saying, "No matter what you do, it won't really count because you'll always be different . . . you're not a proper competitor."

Negative age vibes come in many different disguises, and Pattern Breakers must be prepared to detect them and reject them. Roughly described, negative age vibes are any statements or implications to the effect that the target is anything other than a full participant in the mainstream of life. In short they make you want to bite your cheeks.

A common cover-up for a variation on the Ultimate Age Put-down includes references to a parent or grandparent of the perpetrator. Pattern Breakers who participate in activities largely populated by younger persons must constantly be on the alert for this kind of put-down. If immediate action to purge oneself of the harmful vibes is not taken, the day could come when the activity could erroneously appear to be "just for young folks." As an illustrative scenario, Sally—well over forty and an ardent motorcyclist, having racked up thousands of miles in the past couple of years—is at a club gathering for people who share her enthusiasm for the sport. Several hours have been spent together . . . a banquet has been enjoyed and speeches have been listened to . . . booths with the newest equipment have been visited . . . the atmosphere has been one of total camaraderie. Most of the motorcyclists are younger than forty, but age seems quite irrelevant in light of the common bond. Sally is talking with a club member, exuberantly describing her latest trip, when her listener says, admiringly, "My mother used to ride a motorcycle, but she never got as good at it as you have!"

Scratch common bond . . . scratch feeling of camaraderie. Sally is extracted by verbal projectile from the group and deposited abruptly on a planet reserved for mothers.

The negative age vibe that comes camouflaged as a joke is probably the easiest to deal with. Pattern Breakers, because they refuse to play the stereotyped roles of Ma and Pa rocking away on the front porch, are the most likely candidates for this kind of vibe. A typical setting is a moonlit evening ideal for a romantic outing. As Lawrence and Paula, arms entwined, stroll along the edge of the lake, they meet two younger friends, likewise entwined and strolling. A voice from the direction of the younger couple calls out, "Hey, where are you two kids going?" This seemingly innocuous question carries, in fact, a destructive message to the effect that Lawrence and Paula are entirely too old and dried up to have any amorous feelings, and that if they think otherwise, it's a deviation from the normal behavior of someone their age. In other words, it is not the compliment it appears to be, no matter how near and dear to them the perpetrators may be. The perfect riposte for an attack of this nature is along the lines of the Boomerang Parry: "We're going for a romantic moonlight walk . . . where are *you* two kids going?" The boomerang is now back in the hands of the guilty, who is probably thinking, and quite correctly, "But I'm not a kid!"—a thought that could be truthfully echoed by everyone present.

The Boomerang Parry can be used, with slight variation, for

fending off any joke-coated negative age vibe. For example, the target has just scrambled up a ladder, and a younger person, following behind, laughs, "You got up that ladder like a four- year-old!" The target replies, "*You* got up that ladder like a four-year-old, too! How do you keep in such good shape?" Chalk up another victory, albeit small, in the battle to gain equality, but most important, rest assured that the subconscious mind did not record the defeating information that "you may get up ladders as nimbly as a kid but, like it or not, you are an old person and old people are supposed to be carried up ladders in baskets."

Some of the cruelest negative vibes are not necessarily related to age. They are dealt out to Pattern Breakers, young and old, in an attempt to keep them from leaving a mediocre existence and reaching for something better. True, the perpetrators are usually speaking from their own insecurity and fear, but we cannot ignore the fact that there is a vicious effort under way to cut the target down to size. When faced with a hubbub of negative indoctrination, prospective Pattern Breakers take one of three routes: they become experts in ignoring what people say, they succumb and abandon their plans, or they become Closet Pattern Breakers.

If one is to believe in reincarnation, Jean showed every sign of having lived another life. Widowed at the age of fifty, she decided to return to her former career as bookkeeper, save enough money, and then indulge a fantasy she had entertained since childhood—to live and work in Japan. The Orient had always been an important part of her life: her furniture was Oriental in style; she had taken classes in Japanese and Chinese cooking and was known for the exotic meals she served to guests; around the house her favorite clothes were kimonos, "coolie" jackets, black cloth sandals. She had studied the Japanese language and planned to become proficient enough to work as a bilingual bookkeeper in Tokyo. She had even taken a vacation trip there to look the job situation over. As the time for her Big Change came closer, she was brimming over with excitement and, quite naturally, shared all the details with her friends and relatives.

Jean's son and daughter, both married, were supportive. Though they regretted the coming separation, they had plans to take their families over to visit their adventuresome mother. Support from other areas was almost nonexistent, with admonitions ranging from, "What if you should get sick so far from home?" to downright hostile utterances such as, "Why do you want to live so far from the U.S.?" and "Why would anyone want to live so far from their children and grandchildren?"

We saw Jean a few months before she was to make her move. She was more subdued than we had ever seen her, and fearing that she had cancelled her plans, I asked, "Well, tell us what's new . . . when do you leave for Japan?"

"In two months," she said quietly, "but I've quit talking about it to anyone. Friends," her intonation gave a wry sound to the word, "can be very strange . . . instead of being happy for me, they always came up with some sort of negative remark. Well, that's all in the past because I never mention the subject anymore, and neither do they. They probably think I've changed my mind."

We weren't really surprised by Jean's reaction; we had seen it happen before. Surrounded by negative vibes, she had taken a sensible path; she had become a Closet Pattern Breaker.

All cases are not as extreme as Jean's. The fact that she didn't have a mate certainly made her more vulnerable, since two individuals bent on the same mission are harder to shoot down. But even though the excessive verbal flak may be missing, most Pattern Breakers report a definite withdrawal of some of the people they know. When Tom and I announced our plans for the live-aboard life, we observed this phenomenon and finally decided that we had discovered a test for determining who our real friends were. Those who were elated for us outnumbered our detractors, but in the beginning it was hurtful to note that many people we sincerely liked either did not seem the least bit interested in this big event in our lives or were patently turned off by any reference to it. It was as if our actions were somehow sitting in judgment against their own life-styles—a conclusion that was far from the truth. In fact, throughout our transition from land to sea, we were regularly going to great lengths to explain that the boating life was full of hassles of all kinds, but that we personally were attracted by the many compensations. One can try to analyze the causes of all the poor reactions—envy, insecurity, low self-image. Viewed from any angle it's a sad sight, and we have to feel that a better world would surely cheer the adventurer on. Because we have to live with reality, however, Pattern Breakers must be prepared to ignore all words and attitudes that are designed to hinder their transition to a more challenging life.

And even when the Pattern Breaker is firmly entrenched in that exciting new life, the shooting is not over. Terry, an English friend who is probably the most cautious long-distance sailor we've ever known, took his wife and child across the Atlantic and back despite the grave warnings of the two sets of grandparents. "It's criminal to endanger your wife and daughter that way," was the gist of the grumblings. Having completed the round-trip safely, with few significant problems, they were back in England telling the assembled relatives the story of their adventures.

After describing the beautiful islands, the placid bays, the long, calm days at sea, Terry remembered to add, "We had something of a blow as we reached Barbados . . . had to take all the sails down for a while."

"You see!" His father-in-law was on his feet in an instant, livid with rage. "I told you it wasn't safe to take a trip like that!"

Terry said that though the story of the blow was told several years ago, it is the only thing remembered by the families back in England about a mostly idyllic oceanic voyage.

Sometimes a walloping positive vibe is bestowed, completely invalidating all the negative ones of the past, present, and future. Such was our good fortune only a year before we embarked on our live-aboard adventures. The setting was provided by a visit to our younger son, who had been witness to some of the seamier moments of my battle to overcome fear of the water. On one occasion when I had panicked, he had been forced to haul me bodily out of a bay. Now, a few years later, he was greatly impressed by his newly brave mother and was generally proud of the fact that his parents were opting for an adventuresome life.

At his house we sat waiting for Larry and a group of his friends to pick us up for a mysterious outing in the nearby mountains. We had been instructed to wear slacks, sweaters, and tennis shoes, and to bring an extra set of clothes. Tying my laces, I wondered aloud, "What do tennis shoes and extra clothes have to do with a trip to the mountains? They didn't mention toothbrushes, so I don't think they're planning to stay overnight." Tom was equally in the dark, and as we guessed at different activities that might lie in store for us, the van arrived with its enthusiastic load of young people, and in a few moments we were off.

The van was purely spectacular. It was silver on the outside, and the inside decor included two cushiony front seats covered in white fur, a longitudinally arranged sofa done in black velvet, and a fake tiger-skin rug. Nature-oriented excursions had definitely not been uppermost in the decorator's mind. Tom and I were given seats on the sofa, and the others just sort of settled in, in various poses of total relaxation. All present had on tennis shoes and long pants, I noted, and random wads of clothing strewn about the van hinted of an extra set for each.

As we wound our way out of the residential area and onto the highway, Larry poked his head around from his seat beside the driver. "Guess what, Mom," he enthused, "We're going tubing!"

Making sure that my face revealed no shock, I faked a calm reply, "Tubing?" The mental image I had of this hazardous sport was of suicidal people on inner tubes, hurtling down streams that were teeming with rocks and rapids. And this mental image now carried a disturbing question: Did my son purport to throw me headlong into that kind of scene? A dead silence had settled over the occupants of the van; the plans for the day seemed to be hanging on my reaction.

I broke the silence, my hand tightening on Tom's knee, with a shaky "That's great!"

High in the mountains, standing beside the icy stream that I would soon be charging down, I assessed the situation. Fully clothed, I would be sitting in the center of an inflated truck tube, my legs lapping over the edge. If my tube should become lodged among those sharp-toothed rocks, I would fend my way out with my feet. The entire course was clearly visible, and from the boulder where I stood, there was a good view of the athletic young man who was giving a demonstration. Watching, as he rushed madly down the stream, bouncing off rocks and getting thoroughly soaked by the cold, churning sluice, I wasn't sure which would be the cause of my soon-to-come demise: hypothermia or a jagged rock.

Tom was obviously "up" for the experience . . . everyone was cheering the tubers on . . . Larry was standing with one proud arm lapped around my shoulders. There was no way out.

When my turn came, it was as hard as I had expected, but—with great effort—I faked a suitable nonchalance. As the tube swirled round the rocks and down the surge of water, the cheers from shore delivered some small measure of assurance that a warmer, safer life elsewhere awaited me. And finally the moment came when I could pick my tube up and wade to the bank—shivering, trembling, but exhilarated beyond belief.

As I emerged into an open spot among the trees, I noted a figure high on a boulder, aiming a movie camera in my direction. It was Larry, who had been recording for posterity the sight of his once-cowardly mother flying down a rocky mountain stream on a truck tube. He was now finishing off with a sequence of her victorious return to the starting line. Climbing uphill—my progress slowed by both the chilly, wet vise of clothing and slippery shoes, my breathing still shallow and fast from the combination of excitement and ice-cold water—the thought occurred to me: If I had never mustered the courage to break out of those dull old patterns, I would have missed this glorious opportunity to play the starring role in Larry's movie.

SIX

SEX FOR PATTERN BREAKERS

Pattern Breakers know a lot about sex. Their research is being carried out every day of their lives, and some astonishing results are emerging. Among other things, they're discovering:

• There is no such thing for them as an isolated sexual act; instead, everything that is happening in their exciting lives becomes a part of their sexual experience, which is ongoing and unbroken. This experience peaks often in what is commonly known as the sexual act, but what Pattern Breakers recognize as the high points of an unending sexual act.

• Sex doesn't keep people young; rather, they, through fine-edge living, keep sex young.

• New patterns with familiar partners sharpen sexual acumen and provide the perfect ambience for maximum sexual development.

Breaking patterns may be the ultimate aphrodisiac. Since sex can be no better than the two people involved, it follows that when the participants are living life to the fullest—with excitement sharpening all the senses—their sexual experience will have the utmost potential. Rather than seeking new partners to lend excitement to the physical act, adventurers find themselves constantly in new and stimulating situations that give the requisite titillating nudge to their sexual nature. The presence of the familiar partner, who is a veritable storehouse of shared experiences, provides a mirror—a confirmation—of one's presence in this exciting new set of events. Arousal occurs; a satiating sexual high point is under way. The new setting may be geographically far from the accustomed paths, or it may be right at the Old Home Place, where life-styles have been radically changed by the adoption of innovative patterns. The important element is that the people involved are living challenging, constantly changing lives.

Vacation trips, with motels and hotels in the scenario, have long been a reliable sexual turn-on. Pattern Breakers, who refuse to tie themselves down to the mundane, are continually immersed in the psychology of the vacation trip—complete with the liberated feeling of the hotel or motel ambience—even though they might be working at hard, competitive jobs and living and loving in familiar locales. In other words their spirit of adventure erases the traditional boundary between job and vacation. If a new pattern, whether in the working world or in different fields, doesn't provide this "vacation upper"—the provocative sense of doing exactly what one wants to do, be it hard or easy—it should be traded for another mode; after all, there's no sense in changing one humdrum routine for another of the same ilk. This willingness to change at the drop of a hat is crucial, because just as surely as excitement produces a rewarding sex life, boredom leads, at best, to a prosaic sex life and, at worst, to impotence and frigidity.

In the boating life, people are more open to the scrutiny of others than is true in most other life-styles. And there's a lot of spectacular sex taking place between partners who are long past their middle age. Nick and Charlotte live on a forty-foot sloop that for several months of the year moves from one scenic anchorage to the other in the U.S. Virgin Islands. They're in their late sixties and are adventurers to the core, leaving the Virgins every year for some kind of exciting trip—to the Bahamas, Bermuda, the Dominican Republic, Haiti, or down the Leeward and Windward island chains all the way to Venezuela. Back in their old haunts they always anchor a good distance from other vessels, and after their usual busy day of hiking a mile or so along narrow roads to the nearest store, snorkeling around neighboring reefs, or dinghying to interesting cays and coves, they often turn down evening invitations to other boats, in order to retire early. The flicker of candlelight through their cabin windows and the strains of love songs from their tape collection deliver a clear-cut message to the anchorage that Charlotte and Nick enjoy a sensational sex life.

In any setting it is impossible to conceal for long the signs of a blissful sex life—the unconscious touching, the withdrawal from the group to look at a view together, the overall impression that there's "something going on." None of these signs are unusual among pattern-breaking couples, who carry their adventuresome spirit into their sexual experiences. These shrewd men and women don't need a new partner in order to find excitement; instead they know that the consummate enjoyment of sex is to be found with one's longtime partner. Furthermore, they don't need manuals to help them discover new positions and techniques. They are explorers by nature, and their sexual excursions often take them to situations that would be mind-blowing to younger people. And the major secret that Pattern Breakers know but seldom talk about is that there are two definite levels of sex: Simple Sex and Sex Beyond Orgasm.

Emphasis on Simple Sex, in the media, in the whole thrust of the modern world, has cut sexual expectations short for a large segment of the population. Experimentation with different partners reinforces the lie that Simple Sex—that is, nothing but the physical act plus short-term emotional and mental connotations—is the complete sexual diet that we can expect. Signs of these slim pickings can be spotted in the statement often heard when couples break up: "We just couldn't get along . . . it wasn't our sex life, though. Sex was great!" It is clear that these unfortunates had never experienced Sex Beyond Orgasm, and sad to say, they don't even know what they've missed. In terms of personal fulfillment Simple Sex isn't very much better than masturbation.

In the greatly-to-be-desired Sex Beyond Orgasm, we witness the ongoing and unbroken sexual experience. Ideally, many years have been shared with the same partner, and most certainly, the participants must be enthusiastic Pattern Breakers. Shared experiences of every kind, including the accumulated stores of many years of sexual high points, combine to form the theme, so to speak, of the overall sexual experience—for each couple, a unique theme that changes and grows richer with even the most subtle change and improvement in the individuals involved. The attraction between the partners has deep roots in excitement about living and in an ongoing admiration and respect for each other. Desire is the natural offshoot—"I desire those admirable, life-radiating qualities I see in you, and by becoming a part of you, I will absorb them." The sexual partners actually begin to gain nourishment from each other, mentally, emotionally, physically, and spiritually, and as their personalities develop with the passing years, the mutual nurturing becomes stronger and stronger. The need to be together increases, the need for physical sex increases, and the demands for satisfying those burgeoning needs spill over into every corner of life. As a high point of the sexual experience approaches, the yearning and need for union are so great that the senses are jolted into exquisitely sharp and fulfilling orgasm.

Life is geared to these high points, to these moments of physical union. Words and actions that appear totally unrelated—even the act of serving the other's most basic needs—are, in fact, integral parts of the unceasing emotional foreplay. Romantic gestures such as a kiss or the gift of a flower are the obvious features of that sensual preparation. However, something so seemingly unrelated as doing a routine job—"I'll finish with this so that we can be together later"—also becomes a part of Sex Beyond Orgasm. In this ideal relationship each is constantly aware of the other, regardless of separation by miles, and the emotional foreplay continues despite distance—"Whatever I have to do today will bring me one day closer to union." When together, the high point takes place . . . the body and the needs of the total person are satiated . . . and the emotional foreplay resumes.

Pattern Breakers have every reason to enjoy their sexuality more as they grow chronologically older. Statistics that have been gleaned as to diminishing libido do not take into account what is going on in the lives of the participants. Youth is a thrilling condition; therefore, young people have thrilling physical sex. Furthermore, their bodies and minds call for frequent repetition of this thrilling event. Conversely, old age is a tedious condition for most people; therefore, these older people have tedious physical sex (if at all), with their bodies and minds rejecting repetition of a second-rate experience. Despite this outright surrender on all sides to the effects of tedium, the fact is that as we grow older, our potential for a richer sex life grows stronger. The younger individual brings to the sexual arena a less-developed personal being, and of course Sex Beyond Orgasm can go only as far as that level of development; the older Pattern Breaker, full of verve and enjoying the benefits of a more completely realized personality, possesses the ability to savor sex on a more advanced level. Both young and old can continue to grow in sexual enjoyment until the end of their lives. When the ideal situation occurs, with partners who have been together for a sufficient time span, the unique theme evolves, built on all those past experiences . . . changing and deepening as the individuals change. Their experiences with rousing Sex Beyond Orgasm make poppycock of the common belief about sex between partners who are of middle age and older.

When two chronologically older individuals are obviously deeply in love and enjoying a rich sex life, observers are prone to comment on how unusual this state of affairs is. If studied more closely, one would see that it is the people and their entire lifestyle that are different from the ordinary . . . that their sex life is a natural consequence of these differences. Examples are Joe and Bev, who had always dreamed of homesteading in Alaska and who finally made the big move when their children were through school and on their own. Everyone thought they were crazy, of course ("You'll freeze to death up there!"), but Joe and Bev just ignored the negative voices, stuffed some important belongings into the back of a pickup truck, and took off. Their entrance into this new pattern took place fifteen years ago, and Tom and I have seen them on three occasions when they have come back to visit their son, bringing with them exciting tales of hunting in the ice and snow, of hanging animal carcasses in trees in lieu of using a freezer, of exploring sparsely inhabited areas. The most memorable feature of their visits, however, has been the fact that although their skin shows the wear of time and weather, the people inside have always appeared to be younger than ever. And there's always the same sexual aura about them—the aura that is evident in couples of any age who are leading adventuresome lives.

On the other side of the coin, boredom may be the leading cause of disenchantment and divorce at all ages, regardless of what the individuals involved may believe to the contrary. The unfaithful spouse is usually seeking someone more exciting—someone to stimulate the libido—to make him or her feel more alive. At the moment of the approaching schism, if both partners would simply plunge together into an overwhelmingly exciting pattern, they might very well find each other exciting again.

Sex and life are so closely interconnected that in a large sense the person who is reaching for more sexual excitement is reaching for life itself. Certainly, there is nothing wrong with wanting to feel more alive, i.e., to have better sex. The pity, though, in the case of infidelity or divorce, is that the richest sensual deposits, with the greatest potential for Sex Beyond Orgasm, are to be found with the familiar partner. The unfaithful spouse cannot be faulted, however, for an instinctive urge to feel life more deeply; rather, the fault lies with both parties to the marriage if they do not exhaust every possible means to break away from tedium and give themselves a chance to experience life and sex to the fullest. The salutary effects that the challenging life has on sex and marriage have their best proof in the fact that divorce is rare among couples who are breaking patterns together. When divorce does occur, it is generally because one of the partners could not completely break free from the old patterns and thus succeed in acquiring a new and vital personality in the new life-style. Sadly, some people insist on clinging to the usual at any cost . . . even the cost of their marriages.

One of the most tragic sights around is that of a partner in a long-term marriage who fails to catch the flame of a thrilling new pattern and proceeds to set the scene for his or her rejection. Gene and Frances had raised and educated their family of three, were receiving a good income from the sale of their large dry-cleaning business, and were free to do as they liked. Gene had been raised on a farm and had been marking time, it appeared, during three long decades of family responsibilities, with the overriding thought of getting back to the soil as soon as possible. Frances had seemed to go along with his plans, but when the time came to make the move, she backed out, preferring to remain in the city in a small apartment near one of their daughters. Gene went to heroic extremes to woo her to the farm, building a beautiful house, installing a television "dish" for her entertainment. As of now she occasionally goes out to the country for a day or so but refuses to settle in. Their visits have continued, back and forth from both sides, over the years, but they're apart more often than together. Frances, who as a thorough Pattern Preserver has no salient interests beyond her children and grandchildren, looks ten years older than her sixty years, whereas Gene exudes energy and zest for living and is always brimming over with pattern-breaking ideas for his farm projects. His vitality has overtones of youth and sex, and women of all ages are attracted to him. A divorce would not surprise their circle of friends.

Recently, at a dockside cafe in the British Virgin Islands, Tom and I began a conversation with a handsome white-haired man who was dining alone. He had just sailed singlehandedly from Venezuela and planned to continue on to Jamaica, where his wife was awaiting him at their seaside home. An American, he informed us that they also owned residences in Venezuela and California. After dinner we walked with him to his sloop, a fine oceangoing vessel in a high-price category.

"You have the kind of life a lot of people long for," I commented, "traveling . . . staying in three different countries for as long as you like!"

"It could be better," he said quietly. "I enjoy sailing but my wife doesn't like it. I go out alone, and she visits our children and grandchildren for most of the time until I get back. I'd like for her to be here with me, taking advantage of all this," he gestured, with a sweep of his arm, at the surrounding panorama of sleek yachts and starlit sky.

As we walked back to Romany Star, Tom voiced what we both were thinking, "How long can a set-up like that go on?" Tragically, the stage was set for problems—an attractive man alone in a world that was alive with romance.

In the boating environment we are continually witnessing the enactment of the same drama, with different characters but with the same major ingredients of a man who opts for adventure and a wife who prefers to stay at home. From the woman's viewpoint, I cannot help but pity the female spouse more than the male; at least he is in stimulating situations that offer the possibility of his growth and development, whereas she—perhaps because it's harder for women to shake off the habits acquired while "sitting on the nest"—will never be fully aware of what she is missing. Divorces are the logical outcome of this kind of script, and the new mate on the adventure scene is more often than not much younger, and therefore more willing to undertake an innovative life-style. It is hard to criticize husbands who refuse to become bogged down in the quagmire of aging. And to their credit most of the divorced males we have met would have preferred that their housebound wives accompany them in their pattern-breaking mode—a fact that refutes the general belief that they are cases of Don Juan emerging "later in life."

On the other hand, sometimes the woman is the adventuresome one of the pair. Ginny, a low-key, stay-at-home housewife, opened a hobby shop after her husband Ron retired from the business world, in which he had been a real go-getter. She is the dynamic one of the duo now, expanding her store, going on buying trips, visiting a large group of friends, while Ron is stagnating—providing the perfect example of what society expects the retiree to be. Ginny is changing every day for the better—her wardrobe is youthful . . . she's into exercise and a healthy diet . . . the many new people in her life bring with them new activities and interests. In contrast Ron is aging fast and often declines to accompany her to social gatherings in the evenings. The ground is fertile for divorce. While Ron, as a Pattern Preserver, has chosen the status quo with all its accompanying boredom, Ginny is busily breaking patterns. Her face, her walk, her animated conversation show the effects a fresh and invigorating life-style has had on a housewife who was entrenched for years in a routine that seldom varied.

There is much to be gleaned from a study of how the unusual affects our sexual experiences. Sex manuals and pornographic books and magazines derive their material from unusual situations: sex in atypical places, from the more standard arenas of living room rug and the bathtub to the more unorthodox setting of the top of the dining room table; sex in atypical positions, ad infinitum; and sex with atypical partners, running the gamut from humans to animals to inanimate objects. These suggestions, though reaching the point of the outrageous, have their roots in a basic truth about sex, which is that the unusual is stimulating, the usual is boring, and when sex becomes boring, the desire for it fades away. Most couples remember some very special high points in their sexual experience, high points that occurred during a first or second honeymoon, on a trip to an exotic place, or perhaps right at home, owing to an exceptional set of circumstances. These memorable high points, as diverse as the personalities of the couples involved may be, have one thing in common: they were most certainly not what is commonly known as "turn over in the bed" episodes. "Turn over in the bed" sex has an honored place on the complete scale of sexual experience, but it's the romantic sex that's remembered best and longest.

Romance is an integral part of Sex Beyond Orgasm, and it is not surprising that Pattern Breakers are dyed-in-the-wool romantics. Romance is, after all, at the opposite end of the spectrum from the mundane, and a Pattern Breaker always shuns the mundane and seeks out the extraordinary. The more grandiose or unusual—the more pattern-breaking—the sentimental act is, the more romantic it becomes. Witness the glorious effects of renting a billboard or a skywriting plane to proclaim one's love . . . of hiring a violin trio of serenaders . . . of showing up at his or her office with a single rose . . . of fixing one's mate a champagne breakfast when least expected. Who can better appreciate these departures from the ordinary than a Pattern Breaker, a member of the species that thrives on change and challenge?

The addition of innovative elements to an oft-repeated sexual situation invokes the romantic mood. The sensual atmosphere created by a carefully selected bottle of wine is enhanced by new and delicate stemware . . . the scented glow from artistic candelabra . . . a just-acquired collection of love songs . . . a bouquet of wildflowers. On the other hand, the more familiar the elements are, the less romantic the situation is—and as romance diminishes, so does excitement and fulfillment.

The adventuresome life opens the way to romantic episodes that are exceptionally fine, and without a doubt memorable. Challenging times, such as when traveling over unfamiliar and difficult terrain, sailing across strange waters, launching out on an exacting project of any kind—in other words, doing things that are demanding and novel—form a contrastive backdrop that serves to intensify the emotions of the moment. Tom and I had just made our first offshore passage in Romany Star, having sailed for three days from St. Thomas in the U.S. Virgin Islands to reach Iles des Saintes in the Leeward Islands chain. Our arrival was late in the evening, and after sleeping the sleep of the exhausted for over twelve hours, we spent the following afternoon exploring the quaint little settlement of Bourg des Saintes—struggling, with our limited French, to read the colorful signs, admiring the basketry and artwork, and attempting to communicate with some of the handsome, long-limbed residents. After climbing to the top of a lofty hill for a spectacular view of Guadeloupe to the north and Dominica to the south, we ambled back down into town. Walking from shop to shop to shop, we broke through the language barrier sufficiently to buy provisions for our evening meal: fresh vegetables and fruits, pastries, and a chunk of just-caught tuna. The food had to be special . . . it was the day of our thirty-second wedding anniversary.

That evening in the cockpit nature seemed to be providing a special, unstinting display for our private celebration—the crescent moon, casting a pale sheen on the calm waters of the bay; the sweeping beam from a lighthouse, serving as a poignant reminder of the sea we had safely crossed; and standing all around us in dark relief against the sky, like giant cutouts, the wavy line of hilltops that overlooked the main anchorage at Iles des Saintes. As we sipped the champagne we had been saving for the occasion, we listened to a tape that had been given to us for this special night. The words drifted up from the darkened cabin as if from a world millions of miles away from this remarkable place—"You fill up my senses . . . like a night in the forest . . . like a sleepy blue ocean . . ."

In this stirring ambience, feeling like the most fortunate two people who had ever been in love, we clicked our glasses in a silent toast to the two voyages—three days over the ocean and thirty-two years through life—that together had brought us to this perfect moment.

SEVEN

PATTERNS FOR GOOD HEALTH

Tom had never looked more energetic and content. Surrounded by the merchandise of a large marine store—spools of nylon and dacron line, cans of paint, anchors, winches, bins of screws and nuts and bolts—his face flushed with the pleasure of the final stages of a job well done, he was taking some last-minute notes on changes he would later recommend to the management. The day before, we had sailed into St. Thomas on Romany Star, and with this consulting assignment over, we would be leaving the next morning to return to a favorite bay in the British Virgin Islands. Jill and Bob, a couple in their mid-thirties, stood with me just inside the store entrance, as we waited for Tom to finish and join us for dinner.

Turning away from the sight of my husband's thorough enjoyment of a brief excursion back into the life of a merchandiser, I said to Jill, "He looks like he's had a busy day!"

"Yes," she replied thoughtfully, "and I don't know why in the world he wants to get involved in all of this again!"

Her concerned expression and words were like a dash of cold water on what I had believed to be a happy occasion. "He loves it . . . that's why he does it," I stammered, "and the money doesn't hurt either!" For some reason I felt I had to justify my husband's seemingly demented yen for using his abilities. I further defended him with a weak, "Why *shouldn't* he work if he wants to?"

Jill's answer was a sharply aimed projectile from the munitions stores of the Ultimate Age Put-down. "Well, Bob and I admire you both, but don't you think you should be just sailing and traveling . . . maybe even taking a trip to Europe? You know how one's health can change; you can never tell what will happen in the next few years!" Bob nodded in solemn agreement.

I could have taken the noble route, remained silent, and flushed all that garbage down the toilet. But although Jill and Bob were valued friends, I couldn't resist an inner urge; the need for a Boomerang Parry was implicit in this morbid conversation. Mustering a smile, I answered as sweetly as I could manage, "Tom doesn't want to be in Europe right now . . . he wants to be right here, working in this marine store. And incidentally, Jill, Tom and I have tremendous admiration for you and Bob, too!"

I could have said to this pair of sailor friends, "This man is healthy, active, and happy. Do you want him to build his life around the fear that he might get sick someday?" My instinct had been correct, however; the Boomerang Parry served its purpose—an argument was averted, and the senders were left in a state of silent confusion ("Are we old enough to be admired for doing what we're doing?").

After only a tiny twinge of guilt, as my friends—perhaps erstwhile—regrouped to one side, I coldly assessed what had happened: Jill and Bob, under a thinly veiled guise of concern for our health, had just tried to hand us one-way tickets on the Graveyard Express, the real message being, Why is Tom insisting on remaining in the mainstream of life? Ticket agents for the lugubrious Graveyard Express aren't always friends; they can be almost anyone alive today—offspring and other relatives, strangers, enemies, and even our unwitting selves in relation to persons older than we are. But one requirement holds fast: agents must be younger than the prospective passengers, and the younger the better. Although the sales pitch nearly always carries gentle tones of concern for health and well-being, wise targets are not deceived. These are cruel attempts to extract them from the mainstream and plop them down on coddled excursions to any place in the world other than a place of energetic undertakings.

Permissible stops on the Graveyard Express line are tours and trips of any kind, as long as they include being cared for and waited on; gardening, as long as it doesn't become commercial; card playing, if bedtime is early enough; church, clubs, lodges, societies, and visits with friends; having lunch and early dinners out (you shouldn't be on the streets after dark); walking, as long as you don't break into a run; volunteer work such as answering phones; and the most permissible and acceptable of all, watching television and reading or, incongruously, cooking and serving banquet-size spreads—which would exhaust a hotel chef—for family gatherings at the Old Home Place. Home, in fact, is the Terminal Station (no pun intended), and it's hoped that passengers won't be chugging about too much and will be spending most of their time within those walls that are so safe and above all so far from the mainstream.

Permissible psychology for passengers on the Graveyard Express can be put succinctly: Do all those nice, mild things without delay because Old Time is still a-flying. Other dos and don'ts include these: Don't do anything that will elbow into the ranks of life-involved people. Spend a lot of time huddling over the invisible concern whose popular label is Health (but whose real name is Sickness). Don't walk with too springy a step (that sort of thing can be irritating to the onlooker). Be ready at all times to receive family and friends (after all, why would a couple of old codgers like you need privacy?). Don't talk about sex (coming from you, it's embarrassing). Always be agreeable targets for old-age jokes and assorted put-downs. And keep your eye on the Grim Reaper at the end of the line.

In short the crowd cheering and waving banners along the tracks of the Graveyard Express is sending the message, Never, never lose sight of the fact that you are aging and consequently slowing down! If there were no other reason for disembarking without further delay, that gloomy speculation would certainly be grounds enough. Slowing down and getting sick go hand in hand. If the events of the passing years are going to slow us down, so be it, but we should not be on the firing squad that succeeds in shooting down our very own selves.

Medical science's belief that the mind plays a major role in health and sickness has some interesting cases in point, many of them showing the good effect that change and total involvement can have on physical well-being. An outstanding example is that of Sir Francis Chichester, who took up long-distance, single-handed sailing in his late fifties and did a solo circumnavigation of the world at the age of sixty-five. Before beginning his heroic adventures Chichester was diagnosed as having a serious and incurable lung ailment; his activities during more than a decade after that grim news would have taxed a perfectly healthy man half his age. Challenge seemed to give him health and vigor, since a sickly man could never have survived the demanding conditions imposed by sea and solitude on his now-legendary voyages aboard Gypsy Moth IV.

Cases such as Chichester's are impressive, but because of his much-celebrated accomplishments, it takes a long stretch of the imagination to identify with him. Also outstanding, and more down to earth, is the case of Martha, who was engaged in a courageous battle with cancer from the age of sixty-three until her death at eighty-two. After undergoing a mastectomy in 1968, and through the years exhausting treatment for recurrences, she fell victim in 1984 to intense bone pain that could be alleviated only by strong dosages of methadone, with occasional morphine. By her eightieth birthday in early 1985 a combination of prayer and hormonal therapy had effected a marked decrease in pain. She was almost totally incapacitated, however, by an overall weakness that nothing—neither nourishing food nor medicine—would assuage. Her days were spent lying down, with only a few steps bringing her to a breathless state of fatigue.

Martha was being cared for at a daughter's home in the same city where her doctors, members of a large university cancer center, were located; her three offspring and their spouses were sharing nursing duties. She was deeply grateful for all the tender concern and help she was receiving, but her consuming ambition was to return to her own home, atop a nearby mountain, and to become independent again—to be in total control of every facet of her life. Her doctors were not encouraging; they predicted a steady decline and within a few months death. But Martha dreamed on . . . and laid plans. When still so weak that every movement required intense effort, she began to ready her belongings for a return to a life of independence. Despite her children's insistence that she should take clothing for a brief stay, she soon had every personal item from her room packed in suitcases and boxes. The preparation seemed to give her strength.

I'll never forget the sight of my mother as she left for her challenging life-style. She turned to wave good-bye from the backseat of the car, and the courage and determination in her bearing left no doubt as to the success of her venture. After a few weeks in her independent pattern, living in an apartment at her own home— the remaining rooms had been rented out—her strength miraculously began to return. She was soon caring for all her personal needs—cooking, cleaning, redecorating, and weeding her flower beds—and for two years enjoyed the life she had yearned for. She dined out with friends, attended church, even helped out when other family members fell ill. Her condition and her survival to the age of eighty-two—a stunning contradiction of medical expectation—was nothing less than a miracle, and her change of patterns must have played an important role.

A health crisis often provides the impetus for breaking patterns. Phil and his wife, Ruth, decided to make their breakaway after he had suffered a major heart attack. They sold out a large, tension-producing photography business and took off for the pretty little settlement of Sosua in the Dominican Republic. The cost of living is low in that area—due to the favorable position of the dollar and to the wide availability of inexpensive local produce and fish—and a large group of Recommencers, plus local friends, guarantee an interesting social life. Phil is in excellent health, and the couple's only regret is that they didn't make the move earlier.

Some Pattern Breakers fail to learn their lesson. They undergo a traumatic illness, make the change, then go back to the same old way of life that produced their problems. Alice and Dick sold a thriving shirt factory and recommenced on a luxurious fifty-foot yacht after a heart attack had very nearly taken Dick's life. They enjoyed their new life-style; their youngest son, eighteen years old at the time of their move, entered college and as the months went by joined them for vacations aboard the boat. Two years after our friends' recommencement we saw them anchored in a bay at Vieques Island, just off Puerto Rico. They both looked great—tanned and vigorous; Dick was completely different from the tired-looking man we had known during our land-dwelling days.

They asked us over for a "sundowner" and enthusiastically described the places they had cruised to and the emergencies they had handled, and looking at them, I mentally noted that these were two people who were totally hooked on the live-aboard life.

Dick dropped the bombshell. "We're selling the boat and starting another factory!"

"Why?" Tom and I chorused in disbelief.

"Well," Dick said, his tone abruptly serious, "I want to leave my son a solid amount of money. I started out without a dime, and I don't want him to have to do the same."

We could have rejoined, "But wouldn't it be better to give him a healthy father?" but that's the kind of thing you think, and don't say.

Some would-be Pattern Breakers never have the chance Dick has had. They never make it to a new life-style . . . and they aren't always completely at fault. Ned was an advertising executive who had planned for years his recommencement to a self-sufficient home in the mountains. He had designed solar and wind systems for electricity, had dug deep wells for water, had developed a large pond filled with fish. Kate, his wife, was less enthusiastic about the whole idea. Her rationale for seldom accompanying him on the weekend work sessions in the mountains was, "I have too many activities going on in town." Ned was the money-maker; Kate did a fine job of managing the household and entertaining their business acquaintances, and her frenetic schedule of charity and club activities equaled a full-fledged career. As time progressed, Ned's trips to the mountains became less and less frequent; it wasn't too much fun to be there alone, and Kate encouraged him to stay with her. His work, full of stress, was time-consuming. Weekends usually involved entertaining clients.

Just a year before his projected recommencement, Ned fell ill. The diagnosis was a terminal blood ailment, and he didn't live to break the old destructive pattern. It is impossible to say if the relaxation and fulfillment of weekends in the mountains would have averted Ned's problem, but one can't help but wonder.

Paradoxically, the scene of the most rampant illness is located within the boundaries of the modern medical environment, where efficient hospitals and well-trained doctors hold out the promise of good health. On the other hand, people who live challenging lives in areas of marginal medical resources can usually be seen rushing about, in their seventies and eighties, in the very best of health—seldom if ever ill. Aging and illness have long been linked, and certainly, there must be some relationship. But looking at the record of these individuals who lead healthy, exciting lives, one cannot help but wonder about the complete validity of the statistics. If older people would combine participation in stimulating activities with healthy diet and exercise, would there be some startling changes in the statistics—changes going far beyond what we would logically expect? Is it possible that the continuation of long years of bad health habits, coupled with a traumatic break at retirement with meaningful involvement, could be responsible for far more of the so-called diseases of aging than doctors presently suspect to be the case? If the will to live can often save the lives of the critically ill, then a long-range will to live—in other words an excitement about living—must likewise have the potential for saving and prolonging life. And breaking patterns is the very best way to find excitement about living.

Many people use health concerns as an excuse for not breaking patterns ("I have to stay near my doctors"), despite the fact that the requisites for good health provide the very best reasons for seeking out a new life-style . . . not only in terms of the psychological benefits of change but also because of environmental influences that are crucial keys to a strong body. "Is it healthy?" is the first question that should be asked about a prospective pattern, and that question should be applied to every phase of the new mode. The economic responsibilities of raising and educating a family often keep us chained to a polluted, stress-laden environment. But the moment we can turn our steps to a healthier space in life, where the air and water are pure, where food supplies are as chemically free as possible, and where the pace is set by ourselves and no one else, it seems only sensible to get going as fast as we can.

Our live-aboard life is richly blessed in pure air, rain water that we catch in special canopies, and a good supply of island-grown roots and fruits that aren't treated with pesticides. Another advantage to our pattern is that the stresses are largely of an external type—those tangible concerns imposed by Mother Nature, a faulty sail fitting, or a stubborn motor—leaving little time or opportunity for the lethal, intangible worries that send the blood pressure soaring. In addition to these built-in benefits, Tom and I have included some extra measures that partially compensate for the fact that we sail to many areas with barely sufficient medical facilities. As mentioned before, we hold membership in the IAMAT (International Association for Medical Assistance to Travelers, 417 Center Street, Lewiston, N.Y. 14092), a fine donation-supported organization that provides lists of qualified doctors in various countries plus data on health problems in those areas and detailed instructions on immunization requirements. Our health insurance pays medical costs in most foreign countries, and when making long trips, we carry a policy with NEAR Services (Nationwide Worldwide Emergency Ambulance Return, 1900 North McArthur Boulevard, Suite 210, Oklahoma City, Okla. 73127), a travelers' organization that for a reasonable yearly premium will pay costs of a patient's transportation home, in horizontal position, from any spot in the United States or the rest of the world. An important addendum to our special measures is a medical kit that includes a full spectrum of emergency medicines, including hypodermic injections.

Despite all these plans and precautions, however, being sick in the unorthodox trappings of our life-style would involve a set of hassles quite different from hitching a ride to the corner hospital. This knowledge quite logically serves to strengthen our determination to stay well. Our resolve is further reinforced by a kind of irrational mind-set to the effect that since we have the entire responsibility for navigating our boat, there is no time for ailments of any kind. There are also practical areas to keeping well, such as making sure we get sufficient rest and exercise, eat healthy food, and that we frequent places where the air is purest. Above all, however, we refuse to build our lives and activities around a crippling fear of falling ill.

Like everyone we get our aches and pains, our sniffles and our coughs, but since we're much too busy keeping our little boat afloat to concentrate on these nagging reminders of our mortality, they seem to disappear, from sheer neglect.

Several years ago, at an early December meeting of a study group, a mortician friend of ours was asked to decide on a date for the next session, which was to be held at his apartment, above the funeral parlor.

Without pausing for thought, he declared, "Anytime before New Year's Day!"

Since our puzzled expressions demanded an explanation, he elaborated. "My business hits rock bottom before Christmas and New Year's. No matter how sick people may be, they usually manage to hang in until after the holidays. Business really gets bad . . . but man, does it ever pick up after New Year's Day!"

After the rather nervous laughter had come under control, our group proceeded to vote unanimously to make every day a holiday and to drive all morticians, including our friend, into instant bankruptcy—which is, incidentally, exactly what Pattern Breakers are trying to do.

EIGHT

THE FINANCIAL ANGLE

Pattern Breakers are seldom drawn to packaged, price-tagged experiences; instead they find their enjoyment in the kind of benefits that can't be bought—the challenging life-styles they have made for themselves and the company of the interesting people they meet along the way. A steady diet of expensive hotels, restaurants, and nightclubs would be starvation rations for a real adventurer. In a sense the special needs of Pattern Breakers make them the true inheritors of the Earth. The very best the planet has to offer becomes an everyday part of their lives—excitement, romance, nature's beauties, friendships that are honed on the whetstone of honest interaction, with no relationship to money or to status of any kind. Pattern Breakers do not attempt to buy happiness; they use money to fill basic needs, and happiness is a natural result of their vigorous life-styles.

Pattern breaking may be the world's greatest equalizer in terms of finances, and oftentimes—as in a pattern that is closely attuned to nature—people of low income far outstrip the wealthy participant in enjoyment. On a recent trip to the States we took a long Sunday drive with friends through the Great Smoky Mountains, a rich largesse that regularly draws visitors from all over the world. It was midsummer, and the wildflowers ran riot over the hillsides, punctuating the tall stands of green forest and cropping out from random crannies along the rocky streams that wound down through the campsites. Near one of these wide, partially cleared areas, we parked to stroll awhile along a flower-lined trail. Twilight was approaching, and backpackers were setting up their pup tents for the night; camping vans and pickups were parked, their occupants readying meals on tables outside or cooking on the grills; the owners of two small RVs were also barbecuing. Balls were being tossed about; people were lounging on folding chairs or atop a scattering of rocks. Children chased up and down or skittered pebbles along the stream. At one side an RV of impressive size and appearance—closed up and running its generator for air-conditioning—showed signs of occupancy only as an occasional form passed the large picture window. Its owners, enjoying the advantages of their comfortable vehicle, were oblivious to the drama provided by humanity and nature just outside their door.

A few miles away other travelers who were spending the night in one of Gatlinburg's luxury hotels were missing even more of the mountain experience; their day in all that beauty—like ours—had been a matter of viewing nature, rather than becoming a part of it. Going down the scale from the standpoint of money invested in the expedition, the lowly backpackers, sleeping that night on Mother Nature's bosom, were spending virtually nothing. Yet they were holding the ringside seats to what everybody had come to see.

Only a fool would disclaim the advantages of financial wealth, but there's no doubt about the fact that in almost all environments money insulates the possessor from gut-level contact with people and nature. Illustrations of this truth are enacted almost every day around Romany Star, anchored in one or another of her favorite Caribbean haunts. As we sit in the cockpit for an early dinner, the scene that develops among the boats surrounding us would provide prime material for any sociologist researching the effects that money can have on human behavior. Bathing-suited occupants of the very small live-aboard craft dive into the crystalline waters for their evening bath . . . lather their hair, then disappear under the surface to rinse it off . . . play games with a great deal of splashing and hilarity . . . then emerge to dry off atop their cabins. Simple meals are then prepared inside on a kerosene burner, or the barbeque grills appear . . . curls of smoke ascend. Stale bread is tossed to the hovering terns in order to distract them from the succulent feast that is being prepared. Dinner is eaten outside, and later, when night falls, the cockpit bunks will be fully in use, their occupants treated to an overhead canopy of bright stars, or in the case of rain, sent scurrying to a more cramped, but drier spot inside. The next morning teeth will be brushed on deck . . . conch will be searched for or fish will be caught . . . clothes will be washed in salt water, rinsed in just a touch of fresh, then hung to flap on the lifelines . . . boat bottoms will be scraped, and sails spread out on the sandy beach for patching and restitching . . . dinghies will be vigorously rowed to and fro by the serious budget-watchers, or motored by the more affluent. People will always be meeting new people . . . help and ideas will be exchanged . . . friends—sometimes for a lifetime—will be made.

And most important, the sunrises, heralded by warm rays upon sleeping bodies, will nearly always be the personal property of these lucky owners of very small boats.

A step up the financial ladder, on the medium-size craft, such as Romany Star, people are outside for the cocktail hour. The evening meal has probably been cooked on the efficient gas range and more often than not, will be eaten on the roomy teak or mahogany table inside . . . freshwater showers have been taken . . . comfortable bunks will preempt sleeping in the cockpit under the stars (though a square of stars can be glimpsed through the open hatch) . . . the dirty clothes will be saved for a laundress, and no trips will be made to repair sails on the beach . . . they'll be reserved for the sail maker. Couples and their guests will be seen outside less often than on the smaller boats, but they will appear off and on during the day for various chores and water sports. A lot of time, however, may be spent in the attractive confines of the cabins.

At the top of the money ladder, on one or two luxury yachts swinging at anchor in the deeper area of the bay, the occupants are seldom seen on deck before or beyond the cocktail hour. A tender rushes them away for swimming and snorkeling expeditions . . . meals are served inside by uniformed crew . . . after-dinner drinks are enjoyed in the luxurious main salon . . . television is viewed . . . generators hum throughout the night and day to provide air-conditioning to the enclosed cabins. Contact with people outside the protected environment of the yacht seldom occurs. The scene is one of sybaritic comfort, no challenge, and only carefully measured exposure to the elements—hardly Thoreau's idea of growing wild according to nature. And certainly not a suitable setting for a spirited Pattern Breaker!

The perfect formula for pattern-breaking success would include challenge, involvement with people, and close contact with nature. A financial base that eliminates worries is necessary, but strangely enough the trappings provided by a great deal of money can screw up the whole undertaking. A good example was provided by a television personality, his wife, and children who left the States to live and cruise on a luxurious, crewed yacht. They planned to explore various spots and just generally enjoy themselves. The venture soon ended in failure; they found that even a large yacht can be close quarters and that trying to have fun all day can become boring. Utter misery ensued, and the family sold the yacht and returned to land. An experienced observer could have told this unfortunate family that they had slight chances for success. On the other hand, hundreds of families with limited income are happily cruising all over the world today. The children put in lots of study time, do their chores, and make new friends in every port. There is no paid crew, and everyone over the age of five is absolutely essential to carrying on the shipboard routine. Life is purposeful and challenging. There's lots of time for fun, but not so much time that swimming, snorkeling, and sailboarding can become boring.

Greatly to be admired are the very wealthy who succeed in becoming true Pattern Breakers. Since genuine pattern breaking implies a total change in life-style, and since the accoutrements of the wealthy mode are basically the same in any corner of the world, these venturesome folks share many of the problems of the camel struggling through the eye of a needle. Many have broken patterns in one field or another, such as in industry or politics, but few have completely immersed themselves in new and challenging life-styles. Exceptions may be found among those who have become, for example, adventurers on a grand scale (explorers, mountain climbers, solo circumnavigators), as well as writers, musicians, or painters.

There is a happy corollary to the fact that money often insulates its owners (possibly, former Pattern Breakers, themselves) from people, nature, and challenging experiences, and that corollary is that breaking patterns doesn't usually require a great deal of money. How much money must be had in the new life-style depends on the makeup of the individual involved, and his or her entire lifetime pours into that makeup.

The psychological need for just a few extra dollars will often entrap a person in a potentially destructive situation. Steve is a forty-year-old geologist, father of two teenagers, who has worked for several years in an area where his duties are particularly stressful. His wife confided that his blood pressure, for sometime at a dangerously high level, dropped dramatically during a recent two-month assignment in Hawaii. A change in pattern is clearly indicated but Steve has no plans for seeking a transfer. He is presently earning top pay in his field; a job elsewhere wouldn't pay quite as much, and he feels a move would be a professional step down. He prefers to run the risk of stroke and early death. A complex assortment of factors—poverty in childhood, a hard-won education, insecurity about himself—make Steve the way he is and determine how much money he thinks he needs to be content.

On the other hand, Sean, a prosperous Manhattan dentist with a wife and two children, traded big-city living, with its theater and concerts and high-class entertaining, for a low-key dental practice in southern California.

"My kids were growing up, and I didn't even know them," he said. "Money wouldn't buy back what I was losing!"

Now, enjoying the practice of dentistry under challenging conditions in a small town just north of the Mexican border, he gets plenty of time for fishing and tooting around the countryside with his family. From his point of view the loss of the big bucks is of no importance.

Contrastive situations sometimes help us all to better understand just how important, or unimportant, the well-heeled life is to us. Several years before recommencement Tom and I had splurged on an anniversary trip to a luxurious hotel on the French side of the island of St. Martin, in the eastern Caribbean. The cuisine, service, decor, and beautiful beaches had blended into a perfect holiday. We'll always remember it. Two years after leaving the work scene, we were back in St. Martin, this time anchored off the quaint little town of Marigot. We had planned to revisit our luxury hotel, but as the weeks went by, we seemed never to get the chance; our days were too full of activity. Every morning we dinghied to the dock and bought hot pastries from the local bakery for breakfast. The pastries that survived our hungry trip back to Romany Star were consumed in the cockpit with coffee, as we watched the sea gulls dive for their breakfast all around us. Later, carrying sail bags, we returned to Marigot and spent an hour or so ambling from shop to shop, purchasing fresh vegetables and fruit, sipping a cold juice in a friendly little niche where the surrounding chatter of French gave us some good practice. Inevitably, we would meet other visitors, from boats or guest houses, and the morning shopping tour often turned into lunch and sometimes into dinner with our new friends. We met permanent residents ashore, too, and two families from France became frequent visitors to Romany Star, reciprocating with invitations to their homes. Since we were practicing daily with French tapes, I volunteered to teach English to the teenage daughter of one of the families, and she, in exchange, helped us with our French.

There were many Pattern Breakers in Marigot—from the United States and other countries—running businesses or just simply living there—taking advantage of the low cost of living brought about by the dollar's relationship to the franc. They were tanned and healthy-looking, spending a lot of time at the beaches, browsing through shops, and lounging around in the cozy cafes and bars. We made friends with a number of these happy people and found that they were living enviable lives for surprisingly low amounts of money. Some had rented small homes, while others lived in guest houses. A few had cars, while others, like ourselves, benefited from the exercise and pleasure of walking down the narrow, store-lined streets, always keeping a sharp eye out for the small European autos and speeding motorbikes. We even got to know the police force, and these friendly young Frenchmen, in their immaculate uniforms, would often bike out to the dock, where we would pick them up in our dinghy for a cool evening drink aboard Romany Star. On our arrival in Marigot, we searched for ice and finally found a splendid source high on a hill, accessible by foot through a number of yards that were overrun by children, dogs, cats, and chickens, all of whom became our friends. The vendor was a housewife who froze small blocks in loaf pans in the freezer of her refrigerator. We found a very reasonable laundress, too, who had a large family of daughters who loved to be dinghied out to Romany Star; every time we got our laundry back, we would spend the afternoon serving juice to three or four wide-eyed guests who would politely stifle their laughter over our clumsy attempts at French.

Near the end of our stay in St. Martin, we decided to take a van to the hotel where we had once celebrated a wedding anniversary. We went the full tourist route that day—spending a great deal of money on daiquiris at the beachside bar and on a beautifully served lunch in a dining room overlooking a rock-strewn bay. Later we took a walk along the beach, where vacationers such as we had once been were soaking up the sun. In the late afternoon, when the van deposited us back in Marigot, we walked around town for a while, stopping to buy a crusty loaf of bread . . . sticking our heads in the door of a boutique to say hello to our friend the owner . . . waving at one of our young friends from France, who zoomed by on his motorbike . . . helping some sailors we knew, who were loading provisions into their dinghy. Back on our boat, as we watched the last traces of a rosy sunset, we dined on cheese and crusty bread, washed down by unbelievably good and inexpensive wine.

Our experiences of the day had displayed sharp contrasts—the luxurious atmosphere of the hotel, with its efficient staff catering to every need, as compared with the warm feeling of returning to a little, French-influenced town where we had gotten to know so many people, and to this simple meal aboard our boat. Like almost everyone, we enjoy occasional entry into the expensive and luxurious. But looking back on the events of that day in St. Martin, we mentally confirmed what we already knew: the real fun lies in the arena of day-to-day living with people—meeting them on the practical basis of going about one's routine, rather than in the artificial atmosphere of the tourist track.

In extremely underdeveloped countries it is usually neces-sary—in order to secure hygienic food and water—to stay in tour-ist-frequented accommodations; but when traveling through relatively developed areas, or when living there, the most inter-esting times are to be had in the spots where the average citizen is working or vacationing. The economics of traveling and living on this basis are so good that it could be profitable just to close up the Old Home Place and take off. The average U.S. Recommencer has mind-boggling options to break patterns and take up residence in many areas of the world . . . and in the process, stay vigorous and young as the result of all that excitement.

Another of our memorable experiences as full-time travelers would never have taken place at all if we had been luxuriating in an expensive hotel or on a crewed, perfectly tended yacht and hadn't been picking our way through a dusty dockside industrial area in Fort de France, Martinique. Unable to locate the local tool shop, we threaded through piles of litter in an abandoned ware-house toward the hopeful sight of a sailboat we had spotted pulled up to the pier, just outside an open, hangar-type door. Coming closer, we saw that the vessel, tied to a pair of disreputable-look-ing bollards, was in perfect condition—providing an interesting contrast to its surroundings. A French flag flew proudly from its backstay. On the cabin top two young women were giving an extra shine to some brass cowl vents, and as we began our inquiries about the nearest tool shop, four more heads—three male and one female—popped out of the hatches. By piecing together the English they knew and the French we knew, we were able to communicate. Simply on the basis of that accidental encounter, over the next three weeks we became hard and fast friends of this happy crew, who had sailed from France with their sturdy wooden ketch, very limited funds, and a large amount of courage. They had held various jobs back home, and along their way around the world they were managing to devise other means of making money. We have one of their inventions hanging on our salon wall—a hand-painted poster, with a sketch of their yacht and the signatures of the crew. We exchanged many visits during our stay in Martinique—sharing good and difficult times with them as they struggled to assemble funds for the next leg of their journey—and when we left, were invited to a gala farewell dinner aboard their boat, with candles and wine and a cuisine that was worthy of the best Parisian restaurant. We regularly receive cards from them—the latest from Australia—and will always count them among our very best friends.

Since not all Pattern Breakers fill the financial definition of Recommencers, many find it necessary to continue working in their new life-styles. Some Recommencers simply prefer to keep busy at jobs, and all of this is well and good, since changes in work patterns can provide a stimulating way of life. Ashley and Margaret have spent two exciting decades together—always working but managing to be adventurers at the same time. Their field is car sales, and when we first met them, they were starting out in a new city, with the novel setup of a treehouse office next to their car lot. The idea caught the interest of the public, and the two made a lot of money. Always on the lookout for challenge, after a couple of years they moved to another city and implemented another unusual plan—this time a car lot on the peak of a small hill, with a scenic flower-lined driveway that wound round and round to the top. Along the way, in a life that has never been without excitement, they adopted a fine teenager from Puerto Rico, educated him, and saw him settled in a career. Their most recent exploits took place on a year's leave from work, spent traveling throughout the United States in an RV. Their newsy letters to friends revealed that, as always, they were doing things a bit differently—spending big chunks of time in different regions, actually getting to know people from all walks of life.

"Our love for this country grew," they wrote, "and the diversity of origin, the many common bonds, the genuinely good people we met, strengthened our faith in America." They're in Florida now, busy in a small real estate operation, and two young backpackers they added to their RV crew during their trip have become as close as adopted sons. Pattern Breakers of this kind—in the area of the heart—never go wanting for territory to explore.

Jerry and Peg call themselves modern-day gypsies. After living for ten years of their married life in a small town, where they both worked for the telephone company, they took up the hobby of making silver wire jewelry. At first they gave their small, intricate pieces to friends and relatives but finally began selling them to co-workers. Both had always enjoyed travel, and as their finances improved from the jewelry sales, they purchased a secondhand school bus and began outfitting it in comfortable style for weekend and vacation jaunts to neighboring parks. They always carried some of their jewelry along and began finding that vacation spots are full of enthusiastic buyers, whereupon they made a decision that has led them to a major break in patterns. First they installed a small worktable in a corner of the bus; they had discovered that the process they used was interesting to watch. As a result business boomed, Jerry and Peg left their jobs, sold their house, and moved into their mobile shop-home. They now travel over a wide circuit of vacation resorts, producing jewelry that is in tune with the local scene—tiny silver ski earrings for resorts on the ski slopes, shell and boat pendants for beachside hotels, pine cone brooches for forest retreats. The atmosphere on the bus has a homelike quality, and as the talented couple share the experience of turning out one of their fine pieces for the onlooker, lifelong friendships are often made.

Adventurers who opt for areas that are less developed than the United States can nearly always find jobs using their experience and talents; government red tape is circumvented when the know-how is in demand. Looking at the dearth of trained people, even in areas quite close to the States, one cannot help but wonder why more people don't leave those boring routines and take up exciting lives abroad. Tom and I have been astounded by the number of job opportunities that have emerged since our recommencement—offers to me as a teacher and writer, offers to him in the fields of management and retail consulting. We have met large numbers of men and women who have had businesses of their own in the States and have now started more relaxed operations on Caribbean islands. The Pacific islands are also popular with people who want to start a new life. Mechanical and cabinetry experience is in demand throughout the less-developed areas, and since computers are just beginning to be used in many of these places, experts in this field are snapped up. Professionals such as nurses, doctors, and accountants are often wanted, with law being a more difficult domain to enter, since the legal systems, except in locations that are United States–affiliated, are quite different. People skilled in running restaurants and hotels can nearly always find work in areas geared to tourism. The jobs that are hardest to acquire are those that call for no special training, since this type of post can always be filled by someone from the pool of local personnel.

Countries where American business has a large involvement offer adventure and some very sound financial rewards. Many Americans contract to work for a year or so and while there, travel on their free time to neighboring areas; they save a lot of money, too, because of excellent pay and liberal cost-of-living benefits. Saudi Arabia, discussed previously, provides an outstanding example of this kind of opportunity. Jack is a former Air Force hydraulics mechanic, who took his wife and three children to

Saudi Arabia after completing twenty years with the military. This family found that living conditions were very comfortable, and they liked the assignment so much that they stayed for four years. The souvenirs of that adventuresome time—Arabian tables and chairs, paintings, dishes, rugs—plus the Saudi language they all studied at the company's expense, have enriched their way of life. In addition their savings, now invested in real estate, have given the family economy a real boost. Jobs of many types—secretarial, food service supervisors, teachers, and of course those for all kinds of aviation skills—are available in exotic Saudi Arabia.

For Pattern Breakers who do it the hard way—who create a new life-style without making a major geographical change—the financial angle follows the same general lines as in the case of their mobile counterparts. Challenging modes are usually far less expensive than the more pampered way of life. Living becomes so overwhelmingly entertaining, and time is so full of activities, that very little money is spent for entertainment per se; another bonus of the pattern change is that it usually puts the adventurer in contact with people who aren't at all interested in keeping up with the Joneses. The couple who turn their home into a self-sufficient one—raising as much of their food as possible, using solar cells or a wind generator for power, digging wells for their own water supply—will find that after the initial investment (part of which can be written off as an energy credit on their income tax), their cost of living is considerably lower than was true in their former pattern. If Pattern Breakers who return to full-time studies have to closely watch their finances, they can obtain lower tuition at state universities and community colleges. Furthermore, full immersion in student life will naturally result in fewer expenditures, since the university atmosphere calls for imaginative, low-cost socializing; housing is geared to the tighter budget; campus life can be conducted very nicely, and healthily, on foot or bicycle, reserving the gas-hungry car for special outings. Adventurers who become avid ham operators can either buy a conservatively priced rig or can spend a small fortune on equipment. Whatever is spent, though, will be partly compensated for by the fact that the dedicated ham finds his entertainment almost exclusively on the air and at free or inexpensive gatherings with his peers.

The Pattern Breaker who opts for the creative mode, while staying close to home, will find that the artistic life-style runs the gamut from elaborate to simple. A friend of ours who is not only an excellent painter but also a clever merchandiser of his work purchased a decaying mansion and invested considerable money in reconstructing it. The result is a veritable showplace, with antique furnishings, polished wood floors, carved doors and mantelpieces, antique ceiling fans and fixtures. In contrast, another friend, whose work is displayed in leading museums, makes scant effort to market his paintings and with or without money, would probably live according to his present standards—in a simple country house, with interior walls painted stark white and covered with his creations . . . using slabs of varnished wood for tables and shelves . . . with cushions on the floor in lieu of chairs. The artistic way, with its freewheeling life-style, is a good example of what pattern breaking is all about—and little wonder, since being creative is in effect challenging the norm.

"Laid-back" jobs in one's hometown can go a long way toward breaking boring patterns. Since companies find it more economical, in many instances, to hire two or even three part-timers instead of one full-time employee, a lot of jobs are available for people who want to work only two or three hours a day. The secret is to seek out an area that suits one's interests: for animal lovers, the zoo; for flower enthusiasts, the botanical gardens; for persons who love being with children, kindergartens and nurseries; for those who like the academic atmosphere, college campuses; for people skilled in electronics, equipment outlets and workshops; for teachers, tutoring or giving training classes to company employees; for media buffs, television, radio, or newspapers. Airports, train and bus stations, and amusement parks are full of interesting situations and people. The job doesn't have to be a skilled one; the important thing is to gain entrance to a stimulating atmosphere—one so appealing that work will closely resemble recreation. A whole life-style can revolve around a fascinating part-time job, where interests are sharpened and new contacts and friends are made.

Some laid-back jobs are full-time, and though it takes a good deal of imagination and searching to find them, the effort pays off. We saw a good example recently at the cruise ship docks in Miami. An invalid gentleman of considerable years was being helped off a ship by a middle-age male companion who, we later discovered in a conversation with him, was a very satisfied employee. Both were clearly having a high old time, despite the fact that one was in a wheelchair. In almost any town there are some well-to-do people who are interested in travel but need help in getting around. This sort of occupation could be rewarding in terms of travel, salary, and the satisfaction of helping someone live a full life.

If managing or working at a hotel is done in a warm-winter area, this arrangement can provide an authentically laid-back situation for the adventurer who is able to leave the hometown setting. For half a year these staffs work diligently, albeit in beautiful sur-roundings, but during the off-season they have luxury accom-modations virtually to themselves. Some resorts close their doors in the summer, with maintenance work and general caretaking being done during this time; others continue to care for a few guests. Swimming, water sports, the resources of the entire facil-ity are at the employees' disposal, and meanwhile food and rent are free and salaries—sometimes reduced—are paid.

House-sitting in warm-winter spots, where the owners spend only a few months a year in residence, can provide an inexpensive break in patterns, as well as an opportunity to get to know a dif-ferent culture. An announcement placed in the target area's news-paper or on club and store bulletin boards will often bring a response; in some places bank managers assist their clients in finding people to care for their homes. It might be necessary to locate near or in the desired area, become acquainted with people, and then put out the word that a house sitter is available. Refer-ences are of course necessary, and owners usually expect the sitter to pay utilities. Tom and I have had many such offers in our Carib-bean wanderings but so far have not accepted any.

Caring for luxury housing developments in these climate-favored spots can also provide a comfortable and interesting life mode. Usually the caretaking pair are allowed to reside in one of the homes while supervising general upkeep of all the property. Sometimes they do minor jobs, such as painting, and call in carpenters and other tradespeople for more specialized work; often supervision of repair jobs is all that is required. When the owner of the house they are occupying is in residence—a period ranging from a month to the entire winter—they simply move to one of the unoccupied homes. Life can be sweet and economical, with beaches and pools being their private domain during the off-season. To pin down these appealing occupations, it might be necessary to move to the desired region and do some scouting around. From our observations these are nearly always low-pressure situations, with the owners sincerely grateful to have responsible people keeping an eye on their investment. And here again—sadly for the non–Pattern Breakers involved—the low-income adventurers are often living far better than their moneyed employers, many of whom are still working too hard to fully enjoy their property.

For Pattern Breakers with a penchant for cold weather, plans similar to the above can be applied to summer resorts or homes in cold-winter areas.

On the boating scene many Recommencers become active in the charter business, taking parties out for luncheon day-sails or—as a more arduous undertaking—for cruises of a week or more. None of this work is easy, since meals and boat maintenance are a big part of the scene, but most of those who opt for this life-style find it rewarding in terms of income and the opportunities for meeting people. Another type of situation, available to the person who knows something about boat upkeep, calls for watching over a vessel—cleaning, doing minor repairs, running the motor for a while every day—while the owner is absent; the person who reads and places ads in the various sail magazines and/or makes job-hunting trips to marinas can usually ferret out this sort of post. Wealthy yachtsmen employ, in addition to their licensed skippers, crew of varying degrees of experience, as well as cooks, tutors, or secretaries. Again, sail magazine ads would afford the best tie-in. This kind of setup can include a lot of good travel; the crew is often called upon to sail the vessel to different spots—the Bahamas, Virgin Islands, Mediterranean—with the owner flying in after their arrival or at other times making the crossings with them. For people who aren't interested in doing a lot of sailing but who still enjoy the boating environment, marinas offer a wide variety of positions.

The financial requirements of Pattern Breakers are as diverse as their individual personalities, with each house, apartment, trailer, RV, or live-aboard boat providing a reflection of the owner's special needs and desires. Some seagoing couples feel that they must have large, very expensive vessels, while others, including ourselves, are satisfied with more economical, average-size boats. As for the interior, some sailors dote on simplicity; others indulge a fondness for luxury. One well-known boating family found that when they moved aboard they could sacrifice almost everything with the exception of their piano, and proceeded to install it, against all odds, inside their modest-size craft. Before moving onto Romany Star, that kind of impractical thinking was hard for us to understand. For our adventures on a thirty-eight-foot sloop, we purchased plastic dishes and glasses and nautical-looking towels and sheets. Our upholstery was a practical deep beige, our floors the bare, polished teak; and adornments of any kind—since they were difficult to stow for sailing—were taboo. After a time we discovered that although we wanted an efficient boat without excessive clutter, we yearned for an air of luxury inside, as well as some homey touches that aren't at all necessary on weekend and vacation-type vessels. Romany Star is anything but spartan now with her colorful upholstery and throw pillows, brass lamps, small Oriental throw rugs over carpeting, "real" china, crystal wine glasses, designer towels and sheets, and the crowning touch—silver soap dishes. The inconveniences of cooking in a small galley seem to diminish when the cook is standing on an authentic Oriental rug, and the problems of high winds and nasty seas are less noticeable when the off-watch crew can curl up in a cabin that's attractive and comfortable. And surprisingly, I don't find it difficult to stow the breakables during sailing then set them out again when we've anchored. Outside Romany Star looks like the efficient, hard-sailing boat that she is, but inside she looks more like an offspring of Cleopatra's barge.

Most Pattern Breakers who opt for living on a boat find that their living expenses are roughly what they would be in a home ashore, with savings in one category being counterbalanced by additional expenditures in another. In our own case food is the most expensive item; since the Caribbean is our favorite sailing ground, we must pay the price that is exacted for provisions shipped from the States and Europe. Although some areas have fairly inexpensive local produce, we somehow manage to spend most of our time where those costs are high, too. The amount a land-dwelling couple would pay for utilities is more than equaled by our monthly bills for water (bought to supplement rainwater we have caught and used chiefly for bathing, washing dishes, and for general cleaning purposes), electricity and dockage for the few days a month when we must be in a marina, and ice. Maintenance and repairs on a boat can be quite costly, and these are ongoing necessities. Whereas repair of a leaky roof might be postponed by the house owner, a leak in our residence could be life-threatening. On the other hand, the live-aboard couple saves a good deal on clothing; we live in bathing suits, or shorts and cotton shirts, with a few dress-up outfits. We don't own a car and do a great deal of walking, and have only a very small expenditure for taxis and buses. Our entertainment—except for occasional dinners ashore—is provided by Mother Nature. But the biggest savings of all seems to arise from the lack of space on Romany Star, coupled with the lack of available merchandise; there aren't any of those big, tempting shopping malls in the vicinity of our hangouts, and since our vessel is always bursting at her seams, our purchases in the small shops that exist boil down to the basic necessities.

Of course there is a breed of remarkable people—living on very small boats, catching much of their food from the sea, and truly getting by on a shoestring—who would consider many of our expenditures to be excessive. Our hats are off to these brave adventurers; as shown before, in many ways their quality of life is better than ours. Nonetheless, each person sets out to become a Pattern Breaker from the point where he or she is standing at that crucial starting-line moment. And this rule applies in every sense, including the financial one.

For every type of Pattern Breaker living on any kind of vessel, the financial angle can sometimes be unbelievably fine. We always feel especially blessed in this respect when anchored in what is probably the British Virgin Islands' most spectacular spot—Virgin Gorda Sound, a large body of water surrounded by islets and cays and the hilly, rambling northeast coast of Virgin Gorda Island. On the shore of the sound are three very exclusive hotels, built with the good sense of not marring the scenery, with lots of flowers, shrubs, rock gardens, and trees, and with partially hidden wooden cottages scattered over the hillsides. Since only a limited number of rooms are provided, the two-mile-wide sound and its beaches and reefs are never crowded. Some of the best snorkeling in the world lies to the west of this area at the Baths, and for the conch lover, adjacent Eustatia Sound has plenty of these tasty shellfish for the taking. Hotel guests come from all over the world and pay dearly to lie in the sun, sailboard, swim, snorkel, and sail in small boats and to eat and drink in the flower-banked, open-air restaurants and bars. We swim at a tucked-away beach, snorkel around the reefs, dinghy to neighboring coves, and at times, when we're in the mood for a touch of civilization, we dress to the nines and go ashore for a cool drink or an elegant dinner.

The natural beauties of Virgin Gorda Sound have been widely photographed and written about for many decades, but even for regular visitors such as ourselves, the extravagant display of nature there—the shimmering expanse of water, the undulating hill formations, the nearly garish splatters of bright color against dark green—always comes as something of a surprise. From time to time during the day we can see hotel guests leaning over their balcony railings far up on the hillsides, in rapt attendance to this dazzling view they've seen on picture postcards. And squarely in the middle of a living picture postcard, paying not a single cent more for being in this paradise, floats Romany Star and her lucky, happy crew.

REFUSING TO PROGRAM OLD AGE

For every person who is seeking to change the common opinion that after fifty you might as well be dead, there are hundreds of thousands who are acting as unwitting secret agents against themselves and their own kind—slowing down for no good reason . . . parasitically clinging to the time and attentions of their offspring . . . providing full-blown images of decline. Though self-inflicted these aging blows can be even more lethal than those that are dealt by the outside world. The psychology of "Old Age is getting to me," "It's time to slow down," "My children must keep an eye on me," "I'm too old to do that," and even "I'm surprised I could do that at my age," leaves its deadly imprint on the everlistening subconscious mind.

Genuine Pattern Breakers adamantly refuse to program old age. They refuse to stand in the square that society has labeled Old because they know that life is an ongoing and everchanging event, not a set of squares. This ongoing event called life is full of happenings that are, without doubt, always moving toward a conclusion, but the conclusion is not old age . . . it is death. It follows then that despite good diet and exercise and challenging lives, everyone will eventually reach life's conclusion and die. But Pattern Breakers flatly refuse to program a *decline* that leads to death. Instead they program youth and happiness and vigor because those are the qualities they want to hold on to until the very last moment of their lives.

All around us, every day, old age is diligently being programmed. The hale and hearty person who sells the two-story home and buys that single-story one just a few minutes away from the hospital is delivering a potent aging signal to the subconscious mind. Similar signals are sent by those who ridicule the idea of renewing their academic studies ("I'm too old to learn"); who close their minds to enjoyment of everything that is termed *modern*; who limit their friends to people their chronological age and find the younger group boring; who dress more conservatively as the years go by for the sole reason that one shouldn't wear clothes that look too youthful; who follow the same set of habits every day simply because that's the way they've always done it; who spend more time in pharmacies checking on interesting remedies than in music stores browsing through the latest tapes and records; who no longer think it's fun to get drenching wet in a sudden downpour; who just generally laugh and smile less often than before; who exercise more for their health than for the fun of it; who shun bicycle riding for fear of breaking a bone; who bake, clean, and cook for their grandchildren, but who would never think of getting into a gut-level conversation with them; who never argue with anyone younger than they are but simply listen to what the younger set have to say with a smile that declares, "I know too much about this subject to come down to your level."

All-involving pattern breaking is of course the best countermeasure for this insidious business of old-age programming. But even in the midst of the most challenging new life-style, an alert guard must be kept. When Tom and I began our live-aboard pattern, at the respective ages of fifty-eight and fifty-three, we found ourselves sometimes commenting to each other, "We've got to live life to the fullest because there aren't that many years left"—with a cold mind's eye on living to eighty, if we were lucky. Our definition of living life fully included challenging adventures at sea but nothing so commonplace as challenging work ashore, the implication being that there wasn't enough time left for anything but the most grand sort of endeavors or sybaritic experiences. One day we realized that we were indulging in a kind of thinking that could only be described as terminal. Life lived to the fullest must include any experience we truly want to partake of, and if our new patterns include working at jobs till the day we die, then so be it. Furthermore, life is lived and enjoyed by seconds and moments, not by projected chunks of "twenty-five years to go." A moment in the life of an octogenarian should be no different in terms of zest and interest in accomplishment than the same time span in the life of a teenager.

The negative philosophy that we espouse, "There aren't that many years left," often can be spotted in the shape of attitudes about health. After all, poor health and old age are generally considered to be Siamese twins. The person who gaily proclaims, "I may be stricken with an incurable disease tomorrow, so I should have fun while the having's good!" is falling victim, too, to terminal thinking, and terminal thinking is an indispensable ingredient in the programming of old age.

In the macabre process of laying plans for sickness and old age, elaborate measures are sometimes taken. Paul, a newly made friend in his mid-forties, was showing us through his charming home, perched on top of a hill. As we commented on the view from his back terrace, he confided, "Those steps are too steep . . . I'm going to change them to the other end of the porch. Also, I'm going to convert the old garage into a storage room and build a new one on the high side of the house so we won't have to climb that flight of stairs from the car to the house."

Seeing our puzzled expressions, he explained, "My mother has arthritis, and since it's a type that's sometimes hereditary, I figure it's just a matter of time till I get it."

"Have you had any signs?" I asked.

"Not so far . . . but I'm getting older every day, and as I said, it's just a matter of time."

And sadly, given Paul's expectant attitude, it will most surely be just a matter of time.

Long-range programming of old age sometimes crops up at the most illogical moments. If it happens among adventurers, we can be sure that they are people who are still holding on to threads of their past life and consequently have never become true Pattern Breakers. Fran and Mike, in their early sixties, are enjoying their new mode as part-time live-aboarders but have never been able to reconcile themselves to living away from the day-to-day occurrences in the lives of their children and grandchildren. When they come back to their boat after being with their family for several months, they immediately begin planning their reentry to the environment they have just left. Their residence—which they call "our retirement home"—is being kept in perfect order for their eventual return. Nonetheless, the boating life has done wonders for their health; after a few weeks back aboard they begin to glow with well-being. At a recent gathering of friends, which they had reached by dinghying half a mile across two bays and then walking two more miles, we were stunned to hear them say, "Well, we'll soon be getting too old for this life, and we'll be moving back for good . . . so that the children can watch over us." It was hard to refrain from pointing out all the benefits they were ready to forfeit, but words would have been wasted; these two were too busy with the job of programming their own defeat. And no small part of the tragedy is the fact that the very people they love most will be among the biggest losers when their vibrant example is erased by a routine surrender to aging.

An alarming case of old-age programming occurred in a next-door neighbor back in our land-dwelling days. Father of two daughters and a son in their early twenties, Bob was obsessed with keeping his progeny in town. Since his own parents had died when he was very young, he was reluctant to relinquish the warm, happy times with his children under the same roof. They had all three dutifully graduated from the local university, had obtained jobs in that same city, and Bob's plan seemed to be humming right along . . . until the eldest daughter, a fabric designer for a large textile concern, announced that in a few months she was going to be transferred to a higher-paying position in Florida.

Her father promptly warned her that he and her mother were getting old—they were in their late forties—and needed their children nearby in their waning years. To illustrate his plight, Bob proceeded to age visibly—slower walk, stooped shoulders, sagging jowls—and to develop a serious case of ulcers. The daughter turned down the new job, and all three offspring have subsequently married and settled down in their hometown. Bob later had a great opportunity to take a top-level job that would have included occasional travel to South America but turned it down "to be near my children and grandchildren."

Certainly, children and grandchildren are the very best people any of us can associate with, and there is nothing wrong with wanting to be near them. How sad, however, is the sight of parents, or offspring, who dedicate themselves entirely to this physical closeness, forgoing full participation in life's many experiences—as farflung geographically as they might be. As in the case of Fran and Mike, everyone is a loser.

Too often persons past forty or fifty will decide to give up a specific activity and in order to explain that fact away, will say, "I just decided that I was getting too old for it." Since the negative programming can be almost as harmful for the listener as for the speaker, the remark should not be allowed to pass without comment. A good way to handle the situation is to ask, "Do you mean that it makes you too tired?" and if the answer is no, to follow up with, "If you're as physically able to do it now as before, then why do you think you're getting too old for it?" This sort of inquisition can sometimes be a bit wearing on friendships, but it is vital to keep your own keen-eared subconscious in top condition. And sometimes you get your message across. Ted had always loved horses to delirium; although he lived in a flossy suburb of the town in which we were residing, if a horse got sick, it was trucked from the outlying stable to his perfectly pruned and mowed backyard, where he could tend it day and night. His wife and neighbors were scandalized, of course, and the health department was often mentioned in their grumblings, but the horse would eventually get well and would be trucked back to the stable, and the yelling would subside. We couldn't believe Ted the day he told us, at the age of fifty, "Everybody says I'm getting too old for horseback riding, and I suppose they're right." An intensive interrogation followed: "What makes you think you're getting too old? Are you sick? Do you get winded too easily? Well, then, what's this business about getting too old?" We won the argument—or better stated, Ted won; he kept his horses, and his wife and neighbors began to hate us with a vengeance.

The individual who consistently programs old age appears to view life as a vertically placed spiral—very broad and loose and free at the top during youth, with all its far-reaching experiences and emotions, but spinning ever narrower and tighter as it approaches the bottom, where old age and its limited possibilities reside. As people with this old-age psychology are observed, their actions do indeed become smaller and fewer, as if they were playing out an inevitable and steady dwindling that very appropriately will end in death. If the spiral were upside down, it would make far more sense. To surrender the right to live more fully with every passing year is an inexcusable abdication of everyone's birthright.

This vicious psychology of the dwindling spiral is never more patent than in old-age programmers' attitudes toward geographical change. For no good reason many people totally curtail travel after a certain chronological age. The spiral winds down from trips abroad to tours of the United States, to nothing outside one's own state, to no ventures beyond the city limits. Soon outings within the city are reduced to trips to the supermarket and doctor, and the result is a virtually housebound condition. Even at home the spiral continues to grow smaller as fewer trips outside are made and television and reading become the sole sources of entertainment. By this time health has reached its nadir—with inactivity playing a big role—and it is uncomfortable to be anywhere other than home. On the other hand, people who retain an adventuresome mental attitude and who refuse to limit their wanderings nearly always stay healthy longer.

If funds are too limited for flying and if driving is not feasible, buses provide a very comfortable and economical way to go from city to city. Tom and I recently made a thirteen-hour bus trip that was enjoyable in every respect. The panorama of America is viewed through large windows; temperature is perfectly controlled; rest stops give plenty of time for eating and freshening up. Inexpensive motels abound in all outlying areas, and the many new contacts with people provide good pattern-breaking experiences. As long as a person can get about, chronological age is a lame excuse for living on the dwindling end of a geographical spiral.

The dwindling geographical spiral has a twin in the area of dwindling movements. Old-age programmers will mentally slow their steps when it would be far healthier, and completely possible, to walk faster. Also, in the absence of physical reasons, gestures with the arms and head aren't as rapid and expressive as before, and getting in and out of chairs and up and down steps becomes staid enough to properly match the slower walking. This limited action drains into complete passivity, including excessive sitting and sleeping. "Actions Typical of Old People" would be the tag a computer programmer would attach to this negative state of affairs, and the data fed in under "Consequences" would indubitably be "Sickness and Early Death." Research has shown that an angry facial expression can trigger the corresponding emotion. It should follow that peppy movements trigger corresponding feelings, and there's no doubt that brisk movement is good for the circulation, good circulation can produce a better mental attitude, and a good mental attitude is a key to good health. It would never occur to a true Pattern Breaker to slow down; the riveting happenings on every side keep mind and body in constant swift motion. When something exciting lies just ahead, the tendency is to get there as fast as possible.

Social life among chronologically older people can show the same dwindling effect. Whereas they formerly welcomed new friends into their circle, they now, as the spiral narrows, include only a few companions, and most of these friendships date back for many years. Those who insist that "old friends are the best friends" cannot be contradicted, but a fitting addendum would be, "but new friends keep us young." The same feeling of insecurity that limits individuals in a geographical sense seems to restrain them from exploration of people. Unfortunately, they and their old friends are occupying the selfsame ruts and have nothing fresh and rejuvenating—no new perspective on how to get more out of life—to offer each other. Pattern Breakers move in a diametrically opposite direction to these old-age programmers, making a point always of reaching out to people—the more people and the more varied their backgrounds and interests, the better.

Old age and a closed mind have come to be an accepted combination, and as this mental feature of the dwindling spiral manifests itself, a dangerous condition develops. Since no new data are taken in, the brain has nothing stimulating to feed on, no new thoughts are produced, and the mental processes slow down—often to the point of incompetency. Just as our physical body continues to regenerate until the day we die, likewise our mind and talents cry out for the opportunity to continue to grow and change and remain always young and vital. The author who continues to write the same kind of material, the painter who always turns out the same kind of art, and the musician who persists in playing the same old songs deny their minds and talents the right to feed on something new. Patrick, a skillful guitarist in his seventies, likes nothing better than to entertain his guests with some after-dinner music. His technique is polished; he has the ability to play any kind of number, from classical to popular, but his repertoire has been the same for the past thirty years. His listeners ache to suggest that he learn some new songs, but it doesn't seem to occur to Patrick that his talent should continue to grow—or that his audience might tire of the same old tunes.

When people consistently read the same kind of writings, they are failing to explore new styles and new messages, and this failure to explore and consider fresh material makes them close their minds to change in the world around them. Their private world rapidly grows smaller; they reach the point where they don't even understand what is going on. It is small wonder that they get shoved aside in the rush . . . to grow older and die. Shortly after the first astronaut walked on the moon, I overheard a shocking conversation on a city bus. A man who appeared to be in his late seventies was trying to convince the driver that the whole event had been faked, that for some reason the government and the media had wanted to convince the public that a man had gone to the moon. Later, newspaper articles revealed that many very old people had refused to believe this widely publicized happening.

Traces of this kind of ignorance and isolation can be detected every time an older person turns thumbs down on discussion of a topic about which he or she is sure of having the final word. Matters pertaining to morality are a favorite not-to-be-discussed topic. Whereas a Pattern Breaker realizes that interpretations of morality are constantly changing—though basic moral truths remain the same—the old-age programmer takes a firm stand against mental growth in this area. Three decades ago the majority of fundamentalist churches strongly opposed attendance at movie theaters; today, following the advent of television, only the most strict sects follow this code. Dancing, once a sin in Puritan America, is now accepted by nearly all. The rejuvenating outlook is one that realizes changes are taking place and that it is interesting to mentally explore all that's transpiring in this fascinating, ever-different world. Mental stubbornness and isolation go hand in hand with pell-mell aging, so the wary Pattern Breaker makes a point of rejecting anything that smacks of being "set in one's ways."

In order to keep a youthful flexibility, a person's refusal to be set in his or her ways must carry over to every corner of living, including the areas of daily habits and routines. Habits surrounding sleep can be the hardest to loosen up; sometimes it seems nigh impossible to forgo the same pillow, the accustomed room temperature, and even the same bed. The resultant inflexibility often becomes an outright inability to spend the night away from home. This is a crippling situation, and the only way to correct it is through waging a wholesale attack. Sleeping in different beds in one's own home, using different kinds of pillows and temperature conditions, can be helpful, but the best way is to go cold turkey—take lots of trips and disregard those problems. The person who gets sleepy enough will eventually sleep, even sitting in a chair. People who insist on staying within reach of their own bed, or on carrying their pillow with them wherever they travel, are closing their minds to change and surrendering to the rigidity that is characteristic of old-age programmers. The same is true of cooking, eating, and bathing habits and other daily routines. If adaptability is the goal, variety must be introduced here, too, with new recipes; new ways of cooking; different places for dining, such as on the terrace, on trays in the den, on trays in bed; eating meals at a different time; a bath every now and then instead of the traditional shower, and vice versa; a new soap to replace the brand that has been used for forty years; occasional skipping of the sacred hour of reading the newspaper, as well as the hour of watching a favorite television program; varying the times of arising and retiring. The unyielding routines of daily living, which many believe to be aids to their health, are creating the stagnant soil in which the negative features of old age flourish.

Tom and I have learned this lesson through our live-aboard experiences. Before moving onto Romany Star, our lives were tightly circumscribed by a complex network of long-cherished routines and habits. Life on the water has made healthful inroads into most of the monotonous customs we were so fondly holding on to, and everyday's challenges make it impossible for new sets to grow. When living on land, we were virtually addicted to our temperature-controlled bedroom, insulated at night from noise and light, and to our king-size bed with its painstakingly selected mattress. Now we sleep on bunks that are each narrower than a twin bed; halyards of surrounding boats are intermittently clanking in discordant concert with the rasping of the electrical wiring in our mast; the howl or moan of the wind comes through open hatches, and wind waves slap against the hull; at dawn, daylight streams in and the chirping and splashing of birds feeding on fish penetrate the cabin. But we sleep like babies—a profound kind of sleep brought on by activity and pure air, and providing a more refreshing rest than any we ever experienced in the perfect atmosphere of our bedroom.

When cruising "down-island," tranquil bays are not always easy to find, and one of our most memorable nights was spent in an anchorage off the small island of Montserrat. Dead-tired and ravenous after a long sail, we dropped our hook in the choppy roadstead off the west coast and hastily prepared a hot meal of canned beef stew. Ours was the only boat in sight, and small wonder, since the waves and wind made the spot very nearly untenable. As Romany Star hobbyhorsed around her anchor, her mast dipping deeply from side to side, we ate from bowls in the cockpit, bracing ourselves with our feet against the opposite seat. Dinner over, we fell into our bunks, strapped in with canvas cloths that are generally used for the heeling conditions of sailing, and as the boat churned from side to side, slept the sleep of angels. At dawn we were awake to pull anchor and sail away from what would have been an impossible situation had we not already abandoned our former inflexible ways.

Our cold-water showers aboard Romany Star are a far cry from the hot and cold luxury of our former life. The fact that they feel better than anything we can remember is probably because they're such an incongruous treat, out in the middle of nature. Our meals, eaten on the table below, on trays in the cockpit, or in tightly held bowls when under way, are always different, consisting of canned and dried goods plus the food we have been able to secure wherever we happen to be: lots of roots and fresh vegetables and fruits; chicken and fish, including a good deal of shellfish such as whelks, conch, and lobster; bread baked aboard or bought from small bakeries (often using old-fashioned brick ovens); pastries, cheeses, and other delicacies that are typical of the island we're visiting.

A steady routine is impossible to establish, since our every movement is affected by the conditions that prevail around Romany Star, in terms of sky and sea. If we're in a tranquil bay, we're swimming, snorkeling, dinghying, carrying on our boatkeeping chores, listening to music, reading, visiting with other sailors or with friends on land, hiking, or provisioning. If we're at sea, we're keeping watches and relaxing and reading when all is calm, but when the wind and waves are high, we're both out in the cockpit concentrating on our sailing. At the dock we're usually doing serious maintenance work.

This multifaceted life has influenced every part of our makeup—mental, physical, and emotional. It keeps us alert and healthy and ready to change plans at the drop of a hat. When we travel ashore, we rest as well on a sofa or on a sleeping bag on the floor as atop an innerspring mattress. We don't get bothered—as we formerly did—over inconveniences in airports and stores because we're accustomed to a running inventory of inconveniences of every kind, and we aren't picky about where or how we eat. As long as the food is tasty and nutritious, we can enjoy it while either leaning against a wall or ensconced in a comfortable chair. All of this has to be a healthful condition, since the utter flexibility of our reborn personalities can usually be found only in the healthiest segment of our population—the chronologically young.

Life aboard a thirty-eight-foot sloop can often lead to situations that would make it impossible for the stiffest back to be unbending. On a trip through the eastern chain of Caribbean islands, Romany Star was anchored in an isolated, scenic bay on the island of Anguilla, along with a few other traveling boats. For the nature lover the surroundings were perfect: rocky hillsides sloping down to a curving, white-sand beach, crystal-clear water, reefs for exploring. The only drawback in this tropical Eden was the absence of a freshwater supply ashore, worsened by the fact that the usually abundant showers, always carefully funneled into tanks from canvas "catchers," had failed to appear. Since everyone had been reluctant to leave this haven to fill their tanks, a desperate common yearning for a good freshwater shower had become the prevailing subject of thought and conversation throughout the bay. Late one afternoon a patch of clouds blew over the hilltop and toward the anchorage, promising by its darkness and size enough water to add a few essential gallons to tanks—but not enough to squander on bathing. Activity everywhere had come to a grinding halt. The occupants of all boats waited expectantly in their cockpits with prayerful attention to the approaching boon—now a pale gray curtain reaching from sky to sea and exuding ahead of its arrival the fresh, clean scent that only rainfall has.

"I would love to have a shampoo," I said, scratching my head.

"And a shower," Tom added.

The first few drops splattered down . . . a drizzle set in . . . a cold deluge began . . . and in unison, clothes and sticky bathing suits were shed on every boat, soap was handed out, and assorted bodies, dancing wildly about cabin tops, were washed spanking clean.

As Tom and I fell laughing through the companionway to dry off, I sought to appease the twinges from my decorous upbringing with, "I don't think anyone took the time to look at anyone else!"

Tom chortled, then teased through a malicious grin, "But you'll never know for sure, will you?"

My new-found flexibility had undergone the supreme test—so far, that is.

For us recommencement has been the most challenging and exciting portion of our lives. It has been just the opposite of the old-age programmer that today's culture intends that retirement should be. But if we hadn't planned a breakaway—a decisive departure from almost every pattern of living we knew—these years would not have escaped the effects of society's attitude toward anyone who has retired from the world of commerce. Our recommencement would never have happened.

RECOMMENCEMENT

No gold watches were handed out at this company-sponsored retirement party; in fact it was a recommencement party in every sense of the word. The speeches carried admonitions of, "Remember us when you're sailing across the ocean" and, "Don't forget to write us all about your adventures." Conspicuously absent were the usual "take it easy" jokes and the "drop in whenever you're downtown shopping" invitations. The sea-blue cake was shaped like a sailboat, and Tom's good old office buddies dredged up every nautical term and song they had ever heard. The general spirit of friendly envy carried strong overtones of amazement, because no one had really believed we would go through with our offbeat plans to live and cruise on a sailboat; the sale of our apartment, coupled with the fact that Romany Star was the only shelter we now possessed, had finally convinced them. As we stood at the door—happily clutching or garbed in our gifts of bulky flotation jackets, nonskid boat shoes, a man-overboard pole, a fishing rod for trolling—our friends filed past to give us a parting word and embrace. Many said they'd love to someday make a breakaway such as ours—not necessarily to the sea, but to an exciting life away from the routine. The role model scenario, complete with paraphernalia that bespoke adventure, was a far cry from the standard retiree image. We were Recommencers in every sense of the word, and strong messages of youth and vitality were being delivered to our vigilant subconscious minds.

The unlikely sight of Tom and myself cast in the roles of brave people smashed all the myths that our friends had ever heard to the effect that adventurers are different from ordinary people. We were, they knew, the next-door kind of folks, who had just a short while back learned to sail; furthermore, they were well acquainted with my fear of the water and my struggles to overcome it. By all counts our novel recommencement party brought the whole adventuring idea down to earth: if Tom and Catherine could do it, anyone could. And we hoped that our decision was making a specific statement about retirement—that for everyone the event could indeed be a recommencing, not at all related to the semantic implications of the traditional word, those being withdrawal and a seeking of shelter.

Recommencers need all the good vibes they can come by, since our culture makes every effort to throw them a knockout punch. Enforced retirement, with all its negative connotations, is such a traumatic blow that many of its victims don't stay behind to fight; they simply die posthaste. A leading corporation has gathered a grim statistic from the ranks of its retired executives: life expectancy for this group, where years of high stress are followed by an abrupt cutoff in responsibility and overall *raison d'être*, is a year to eighteen months. If this same age group were given excitement and ongoing purpose in their private lives—a recommencement— or if they remained on their jobs, statistics would certainly show a different picture. It is hard to understand why those persons who resist the "slowing down" brainwashing and remain healthy, alert, and able to do their work well are not allowed to continue with the same employer for as long as they wish. In most corporations executives at the very top, such as national or international presidents, are allowed this privilege. And our elected officials, including U.S. presidents—who form the hub around which our country's machinery turns—continue to serve long after the age of sixty-five. The current profligate chopping out of some of our very best resources would only make sense if they were to be used for some better purpose; under today's system of enforced retirement, good and bad are shoved aside to wither and decay. Of course there would be many problems arising from a voluntary retirement policy, but today's solution is robbing our nation of a lot of fine talent.

Retirement is the official announcement of one's exit from the mainstream, an exit that wipes out for all time a long-standing identity. The suggestion of finality, with no hope of renewal, is closely related to the general aura of death. Other countries use the work identity far less often in the social context, but in the United States "I work for Thatcher, Inc." is the standard addendum to "My name is John Smith." "I'm a retiree," a title that covers a broad and largely inactive segment of the population, just doesn't fill the bill. Women who retire appear to weather the crisis far better than men, and the reason probably lies in the identity factor; since in most instances their interests and skills have been divided between home and work, they lose only the personality of the outside job, retaining their homemaker identity throughout life. Pattern breaking is closely related to identities, since one identity is exchanged for another, but retirement follows the definition only to a point—a pattern is broken. What lies ahead—the absorption into a faceless herd of people labeled as retirees—is antonymous of what true pattern breaking is all about.

Since not a single person who lives a decent number of years will escape the stigma of chronological aging, it is astounding that society insists on tilting the working-scene scales in favor of the very young, laying a difficult path for one and all through a major portion of the average career; there's a downright self-destructive tinge to the whole affair. Around age forty the professional putdowns begin, with talk of the need for new young blood, the implication being that in order to get new ideas a company must import new bodies. Our youth-oriented culture—so different from that of China and many other countries—seems to be constantly rushing in fresh troops from an unreasoning fear that somehow the battle is being lost because of age. Age becomes such a weak point that the chronologically older must often go an extra mile just to win the reputation of keeping up with progress. Younger employees—and most of us have been guilty of this—assume a patronizing air toward the "deadwood," and as retirement nears, life often becomes nigh impossible for a lot of good people. The pity is that those difficult years should in fact be the very best ones, in terms of making contributions and winning appreciation.

As retirement age draws close, the friendly banter all points to the common insistence that nothing but relaxation and good times lie ahead, but the underlying signal put out by the approaching event is anything but friendly. The future retiree is being told in no uncertain terms that a functioning part in the company machinery is wearing out, and "sorry, old buddy, but that disabled part is you." In the area of nonphysical jobs enforced retirement carries a heavy suggestion of diminished mental abilities, when in truth it is robbing the retiree of a large chunk of mental stores—most that has been learned in several decades will be largely unusable outside the company's walls. In contrast workers such as mechanics and carpenters, who use manual skills, will probably continue to activate their job knowledge in their personal environment. The business person, even with plans to seek employment elsewhere, will have little use for all those complicated specifics at which he or she has become so adept. And more than knowledge will be lost; all of that interrelating, the fun around the coffee urn, the good times and the bad times—all shared like one big family—a complete life that has been constructed independently from the one at home, will be over . . . irrevocably over. Even if retirees-to-be have convinced themselves that they're glad ("I've given too much of my life to this place"), the fact still remains that their usefulness to the company is coming to an end. Even if they take early retirement, they're still just a jump ahead of the mandatory retirement gun; eventually, it would have shot them down, too. And by voluntary or mandatory route, the effect is the same: the company will send them a pension check for life, but in most cases their input will not be asked for or desired.

The ceremonies with their standard speeches and "going fishing" joviality are over, the parties have been held and the gifts dutifully received, and the great time that everybody has been extolling has arrived. If a celebratory trip was taken, it has come to an end, and—in the traditional scenario—the man who was dependably away and occupied in purposeful activities is suddenly at home all day. At first the feeling is just great for both man and wife—getting up as late as they wish, golf or tennis or fishing whenever the mood strikes, visits with the children and grandchildren, with no deadlines set by the demands of one's job. But as being free from work becomes routine, the problems begin, with squabbles arising from the marriage that was "for life but not for lunch," with too much drinking often following an overwhelming boredom, and with a puzzling and consistently verbalized attitude on everyone's part that the retiree should be happy doing what a man in his position is supposed to be doing, i.e., just taking it easy.

The "who am I" crisis that the retiree is going through is worsened by the fact that he no longer wields power of any consequence—understandably, an upsetting situation—and that although in this much-touted state of joy called retirement he's angry much of the time, he no longer knows with whom or what to be angry. Whereas before, the foibles of his employers always provided convenient objects for his wrath, there is now no suitable opponent other than the stores, which used to be his wife's territory but where he seems to be spending a lot of time lately. Outside of golfing or some other sport there seems to be no common ground with anyone for a good discussion or argument. There is no shared knowledge of the company's shortcomings, no common ability, experience, and responsibility that lift two or more men out of the mundane world and lead them to conclusions that make a difference. His predicament isn't helped by the family's overly protective attitude—a logical result of this documented farewell to meaningful occupation—which makes the retiree suspect that his health must require a great deal of attention and, to be truthful, flat-out worry. Also, there's reason to worry about the money supply because here he is, living in the same general way, with the same expenses—regardless of well-intentioned plans to the contrary—and with a monthly check that has shrunk considerably. And who knows just how bad inflation will get? Ironical as it may seem, at the time of life when all the hostilities of the business world, the daily efforts to shoot him down, are done with—when he is supposed to feel loved and cared for on all sides—he nurses a growing suspicion that it's Open Season and he's the Target.

The hapless retiree, victimized as he may appear, is actually dancing to a tune that he has helped compose. His creative efforts started many years back when he first fell for the line that people have to slow down as they grow older, and have to allow their lives to taper off into a nonsensical condition of inactivity. Following the example of others, he began early on to use his eventual nemesis as a joking excuse for sheer laziness ("I'm getting too old for this kind of thing"). He settled into a set of social habits that were characterized by their sedentary nature and total lack of imagination. This general vein of thinking and doing things had the logical negative impact on his daily approach to the job and on his overall ability to generate inner enthusiasm. The slowing steps and the conversation about the same old subjects—mowing the yard, fixing the car, family problems—were exactly what was expected of him; after all, he was the old man who was on his way out. And all those spurts of "I'll show them what I can do" were recognized for what they were . . . all the posing in the world couldn't cover up the fact that fresh ideas don't come from a man who hasn't changed in thirty years. Small wonder that his company was always reaching out for younger people. But what a pity that all that experience and talent should go to waste when every person has the innate potential for daily rejuvenation. Unfortunately, too, all those stultifying patterns of his social and work mode were draining directly into his life as a retiree.

Avid Pattern Preservers usually dread retirement, and rightfully so. People who are interested in maintaining the status quo have such a diminished interest in the world around them that the thought of living without the inclusion of the familiar job is often enough to lay the path to postretirement death. Other Pattern Preservers begin retirement with enthusiasm, only to find that nothing is the way they had thought it would be. Kurt and Ginger had looked forward to traveling and had laid elaborate plans for an immediate trip to Japan. They would be there for a month, with two weeks in Tokyo and with the rest of the time spent touring outlying areas. We saw them on their return, and because we knew the couple well, we were not surprised to see that they were more deflated than pleased about their trip.

"There really wasn't anything to see," Kurt sighed. "The buildings were nothing compared to what we have here in the States."

"And the stores were a big disappointment," Ginger added. "I didn't see anything I wanted to buy."

Kurt and Ginger had failed to change their old, uninspired attitudes before they went to Japan. Their trip hadn't broken a single internal pattern, so it was natural that in a land of fascinating customs and sights, they couldn't find one thing that was truly interesting.

Pattern Preservers' resistance to change often turns into an outright masochism. Natalie, divorced for many years, had decided to make a cruise ship excursion her big retirement fling. Since these trips are noted for their success in bringing singles together, she had pinned a lot of hopes on what was for her an expensive investment. We had met her on a trip to New England and in response to a postcard, were waiting at the Charlotte Amalie dock in the U.S. Virgins when the mammoth pleasure palace glided in, its railings lined with excited people. Hoping to see our friend come down the gangway on some handsome gentleman's arm, we were doomed to disappointment; instead she hurried nervously down, alone, and over to the shady spot where we were waiting.

"How's it going?" I queried, after the welcoming hugs and kisses had been dispensed with.

"Not so hot!" she said. "And by the way, could you take me to a good supermarket?"

Since cruise ships are famous for their cuisine, we reacted in chorus with, "Are you kidding?"

"No, I'm not," she said with a bothered grimace, "All that weird food is absolutely driving me nuts . . . I just can't wait to buy some of the things I'm used to!"

We took her to a supermarket, and she purchased cans and jars of the most ordinary food items that can be imagined, along with a can opener and paper plates. Only then did she relax enough to do some mildly enthusiastic sightseeing on the scenic island of St. Thomas. As wholesome a woman as Natalie is, she'll find a mate only in the person of another Pattern Preserver whose eccentricities exactly fit hers—a tall order, to be sure.

George was a Pattern Preserver whose principal interest in life, outside of his job, was golf. When asked about what he would do on retirement, he always answered, "Just travel around everywhere, playing on different golf courses . . . I could spend the rest of my life that way!" Before retiring, he and his wife took a trip to Spain, where he played on a course that is world famous. They stayed in luxurious accommodations and just generally gave their retirement plans a good test.

Tom saw him shortly after his return and said, "You must have had a great time playing golf in Spain!"

With an unhappy frown George replied, "The hotel was fine, but believe it or not, while I was playing on that course, all I could think of was that I could be doing the very same thing on my own club course right here in Fort Lauderdale! Man, do I dread retirement . . . I don't know what I'm going to do with all that free time."

His other problem was one shared by many: he and his wife loved each other but couldn't bear to spend one whole day together. She had her luncheons and clubs, and he had his work and golf. The thought of what lay ahead when that job came to an end gave them both cold chills. Strangely, the precious gift of time can ruin lives of the typically unimaginative Pattern Preserver.

Gail was a Pattern Preserver married to Jed, who enjoyed breaking patterns. Although her conservatism held him back, he at least managed to get some interest into his work life by securing a job that entailed living for periods of two or three years in one city, then moving to another. Gail's survival mode under this assault on her desire to stay put was quite inventive: she created a bearable environment for herself by loudly expressing hatred for the city she was living in, extolling the virtues of the city she had lived in last, and talking incessantly about how good life would probably be on the next move. To her credit she managed to hang in until retirement time, and now, tucked away in the meticulously built and outfitted home where she'll be for the rest of her life, the habits of the past prevail, and all the cities she once lived in outshine the one in which she has settled. Unfortunately, unless she becomes a Pattern Breaker, there's no next move to anticipate . . . at least not on this planet.

For Recommencers the end of the nine-to-five routine is a happy occasion, not because they dislike their jobs, but because something far more thrilling lies ahead. That has always been their mind-set: as exciting as today is, tomorrow will be even more so. Mandatory retirement, unjust as it is, has no negative impact on this different species of people; instead, Recommencers have learned to turn what could very well be a killer blow into a healthful event, i.e., a facilitator for their important personal plans. They persist in puzzling everyone around them because they just don't fit the pattern of other chronologically aging people. They are always enthusiastic about their jobs, and the best ideas in the company come from them. Their gusto and ability derive from their mental attitude, which of course is tied into the whole spectrum of the interesting lives they are leading. When they bounce onto the work scene, they exude an aura of success and general well-being; to call them deadwood at any age would be ludicrous. When they finally insist on "retiring"—usually well before sixty-five—their retirement forms are delivered by reluctant hands, and when the eve of what they know to be their recommencement arrives, their ambitious plans for the future spread such a thick layer of foam around the work scene that not a single negative vibe can spark. Everyone around them just wishes they could be Recommencers, too.

Like all genuine Pattern Breakers, Recommencers are also pattern creators. No two Recommencers ever follow the identical road to self-realization; there will always be differences in their methods or in their private view of what they are doing. Even if they decide to work again during recommencement, their jobs will not be a mere continuation of what they've been doing for the past thirty or forty years—they'll always manage to do things a bit differently.

Rolf, who had started a small housecoat factory when he was chronologically young, building it through the decades into a big business, had deeply enjoyed the few times he had been able to fill in for one of his salesmen and travel to foreign countries with his sample racks, making the deals through person-to-person contact with buyers. He also enjoyed deep-sea fishing, but hadn't had much time to indulge in it during those busy years of full-time work. Upon his recommencement, when he turned the reins over to a son, he bought a house with a small dock on a Miami canal, maintained a fishing boat there, and started fishing several times a week. This steady routine soon became boring, and he began to dream of the fun he had had on the road. Against the strong objections of wife, children, and friends, he went to work as a traveling salesman for his company and today is a glowing example of someone who delights in life. His wife finds she likes making trips with him from time to time, and they always manage to squeeze in some sightseeing. Though Rolf doesn't fish much anymore, he says he likes nothing better than to come in from a long selling trip, go out to the dock, turn on the motors, and just listen to that peaceful hum for a while. Crazy? Well, some might call it that, but in truth Rolf's case illustrates what pattern breaking and creating is all about—each person's private and creative way to full enjoyment of life.

Recommencement is an ideal time for testing that artistic streak that every single one of us has. It's to be hoped we won't wait till then, but if circumstances have somehow forced a delay in full examination of our talents, the postjob days give us the time and financial support we need to get down to business. Ann is a widow who raised and educated her children by working as a field representative for Social Security. She had dabbled in watercolors since her high school days, and some of her art was proudly displayed in her friends' homes, but she had never developed her abilities past the same general technique that her first paintings had shown. Several years before her anticipated recommencement, Ann enrolled as a night student in the local university and eventually succeeded in graduating with a degree in art. Now, with the time to do what she likes, she combines painting and sculpture with running her own gallery, and even holds low-tuition classes for aspiring artists.

Some people might think that Ann would regret the many years spent employed outside the field of art, but she says, "Everything I've ever done or learned ends up in my work now. This is the right time to be doing it."

Too often, chronologically older people become so isolated from the younger generation that communication virtually comes to a standstill. Since they aren't going to discos and honestly can't fathom modern music and movies, they can't seem to find any common ground for interrelating. The result is an alienation that often turns into hostility—on both sides. Recommencers don't fall into this unhappy trap. Their common ground with younger people is a mutual love for excitement. Their exploits and life-styles often succeed in outshining those of individuals half their ages, and wherever they are, the younger segment can always be found, too.

A septuagenarian friend of ours—a recommenced personnel-relations consultant who dabbles in poetry, painting, music, horseback riding, philosophy, religions of the world, languages, and scuba diving (to name a few of his interests)—always describes himself as a "rejuvenated teenager." Wherever he is, the very young, the middle-aged, and the very old manage to seek him out, and in his presence the shared love for exciting pursuits provides a perfect common ground. His only problem is that there aren't enough hours in the day for all his involvements. The walls, floors, and furniture of his living room and bedroom are crowded with books, musical instruments, records, tapes, and paintings. His car is littered with language and music tapes; his kitchen has books propped up all around for study while he waits for the pot to boil or the coffee to perk; the bathroom supports a complete library, plus tape recorder. Jamming several lifetimes into one, he puts to shame the monoexistences that most people experience.

Although anyone alive today can make a complete about-face at this very moment, the fact is that many Recommencers date a long way back as Pattern Breakers. A likely success as a Recommencer is the man or woman at the office who loves horses and has pictures of them on walls and desk . . . or keeps a trailer near the beach . . . is building a house almost singlehandedly on weekends and at night . . . rides a motorbike to work in all kinds of weather, or insists on walking several miles to get there . . . has a hobby that few people know much about, such as collecting old bottles or raising a garden Chinese-style . . . flies small planes or sails, or is building an airplane or boat in the backyard . . . travels to unheard-of places at vacation time . . . collects and redoes antique cars and actually drives an eye-catching model to work . . . has an unconventional assortment of friends . . . is always taking some kind of course in night school. Prospective Recommencers usually do a better job at the office than most people, but their daily actions make it quite clear that there is more to life than their association with The Company.

To become a Recommencer all a person needs is a genuine desire to be one, and most defeats result from ignorance as to what that emotion actually entails. I came face-to-face with my own lack of knowledge in the field of "wanting," back in the days when I was attempting to overcome my crippling water-related phobias. At the outset I discovered that what I had thought of as desire had been nothing more than a fantasy with no "arms or legs" to propel it forward. Finally, however, the fantasy became the honest emotion, as the result of envisioning myself doing all those difficult things and enjoying them . . . as I ventured, as often as possible and under optimum conditions, into the intriguing environment . . . and as I consciously used the emotions of self-disgust and anger to address my stalemated condition, plus sheer envy of those who were enjoying what I found to be a nearly impossible feat.

The same techniques can turn the most resolute Pattern Preserver into a full-fledged Pattern Breaker and Recommencer. Just as I had to take a tiny step at a time—down the boat ladder, away from the ladder, and finally all the way to the reefs, as well as that from owning a small boat to learning to love life on the water, and finally to making the transition to full-time life aboard—the would-be Recommencer can start with small changes that steadily grow and eventually build into astonishing upheavals of a humdrum existence.

As part of a consciously programmed reach for true "wanting to change," ventures into change can begin in the form of adopting new food habits, dressing differently, reading books that formerly were rejected without examination, listening to a different kind of music, and widening one's circle of friends to include a lot of Pattern Breakers. Whether working days are still in progress or retirement is already in full swing, the Recommencer-to-be should let everyone around know that a revolution is under way. The expectations of other people serve as a reliable reinforcement of all that is taking place—as long as negative vibes are properly ignored—and establish effective roadblocks against retreat; in the early days of my metamorphosis these roadblocks often prevented me from turning back on the road that eventually led to a happy live-aboard life.

And once the sweet taste of change has become a habit, the only remaining step is to decide in which direction to go. The sky's the limit, but whatever those plans are, they should be magnificent enough to completely overshadow that behemoth of old-age programmers known as retirement, and to effectively program youth and, without question, the "better part of life."

The general air of mystery that surrounds living aboard a boat helped to make our move far more impressive than it actually was. Everyone was so perplexed by our plans that the negative vibes that usually surround retirement just never got off the ground. Because most of our friends equated what we were about to do with setting up housekeeping on a beach or on a space shuttle, or perhaps in an underwater habitat, we encountered some rather singular reactions. The most common query was, "What are you going to do all day . . . just lie in the sun and swim and fish?" When the going gets tough and the motor's laid out all over the cabin sole or the pumps refuse to work or the weather decides to thwart all our efforts to get someplace, leaving us tired and wet in the process, we sometimes manage to joke, "People who live on boats just lie in the sun and swim and fish all day!" Another concern our friends expressed was, "What will you eat?"—not realizing that one eats basically the same kinds of food on a boat as on land, storing it in lockers and iceboxes, or in mechanically operated refrigerators, the variation mainly lying in the different fruits and vegetables that are native to the area being visited. For our questioners who had visions of a boat being an open-decked affair, with little or no enclosed space, a principal worry was where we would sleep and cook. They were relieved to find out that our cabin is quite snug, with plenty of headroom, with bunks that somewhat resemble beds, a galley that has not only an icebox but also a three-burner gas stove with oven, and a sink with three faucets—two connected to foot pumps for fresh or salt water and the other to a freshwater electric pump. For those who asked about hot water we explained that a steaming kettle provided a solution dating back to log-cabin days.

"How will you manage to live in so little space?" was a question often posed as we sat in residences comprising nearly three thousand square feet. We're still trying to find the answer to that one, but the solution probably lies in the fact that since we live and cruise only in tropical climes, our roomy cockpit is our year-round living room, and our natural surroundings are our backyard. Inside the boat the compact arrangement is a mitigating factor, along with the ongoing battle we wage to keep useless items from coming aboard. One of the most amazing questions—advanced by an alarming number of friends, after we had gone to great lengths to describe our plans to sell our apartment and live permanently aboard our vessel—was, "But where will your *home* be? . . . where will you actually *live*?" And we'll never forget the often-- asked, "When you get sleepy on a long trip, will you anchor right there in the middle of the ocean?"

RECOMMENCEMENT

But the most astounding question of all was put forth by a mid-western friend who, shortly after our move onto Romany Star, took her first sailing trip with us—a jaunt from Puerto Rico to the island of Vieques. Since the trip was made with the heavy winds constantly abeam, we didn't need to change our direction, so instead of our usual tacking back and forth, with the boat heeling alternately to port and starboard, we were sharply heeled over to the starboard side for the entire trip. After a couple of hours Meg found it necessary to visit the head—a precarious perch on this particular trip, due to its portside location. As she struggled back into the cockpit, she exploded in total exasperation with, "Why in the world didn't they put the toilet on the other side so a person wouldn't fall off when the boat leans over like this?"

During Tom's final days on the work scene, the air of bafflement that prevailed among most of our friends and acquaintances sometimes caused us to ask ourselves if we were totally insane to step so far out of line with the general opinion. One look, how-ever, at what everyone expected of us—a gentle span of years revolving around a structure we would buy or build and label our "retirement home"—would always strengthen our resolve. For us there was really no choice; bizarre as it might seem, recommence-ment aboard a thirty-eight-foot sailboat was the only way to go.

ELEVEN

SETTING NEW
PEOPLE-PATTERNS

Our most memorable recommencement party was given on our last evening as land dwellers by the local chapter of the U.S. Power Squadron, where we had learned everything we knew about navigation. In the company of these good people we had learned to plot a safe course through dead reckoning (using compass, chart, and currents) or through celestial methods (combining dead reckoning with the use of a sextant, which measures the angle between sun, moon, or stars and the horizon). And we had shared many weekend and vacation trips, traveling fleet-style in our various boats. Tom and I were the first members to have ever sailed off into a full-time cruising life, and our farewell gathering was suitably festive—resembling more than anything a gala wedding celebration. Speeches about our exciting venture were made, and pledges of eternal friendship exchanged; a plaque, which now hangs on Romany Star's salon walls, promised, "Wherever you go the sea will unite us." At the end of an evening of food, drink, excited chatter, and dancing, the floor was cleared, and we were asked to dance to the strains of "Vaya con Dios," as our friends made a circle around us. After a lot of emotional good-byes the party was over, and we drove back to the apartment that no longer belonged to us, to do some final packing before our departure the next day.

As was natural we felt sentimental about leaving that close association with so many wonderful people, but we were sure that distance would not weaken any of those bonds. Ahead of us, we knew, lay a lot of relationships with new and quite different men and women—many of them dedicated adventurers, others living in cultures contrasting sharply with our own. The prime role that all those new people-patterns would play in our recommencement was impossible to envision at the time of our transition from land to sea.

About a year later, when sailing off from an island where we had made many fast friends among both the local and sailing population, another memorable farewell party was given. Songs were sung, tears were shed on all sides, and several of the party guests gathered the next morning to wave to us as our dock lines were cast off. As we rounded the point just outside the marina, a solitary figure appeared on a knoll and blew a traditional farewell on a conch shell. A long time would pass before we would see those dear friends again, but by then we had learned that the appeal of the adventuresome mode we were following lay less in heroic exploits than in the steady stream and unending variety of people who flowed through our lives. Farewells and first hellos are said to someone almost every day, and the net result of this rich exposure to humanity is a life whose interest far exceeds our former expectations.

If we had entered our new life with anything less than wide-open minds and emotions in regard to people, I am sure we would have failed at the outset. Whether the new mode carries the Pattern Breaker to distant lands or is conducted on the old, familiar grounds, the sum total of success will probably depend on close involvement with a large variety and number of people; even the most solitary of adventures are usually highlighted by those precious moments of human contact, illustrating that the undertakings were successful despite a handicap—the absence of others. Singlehanders who circumnavigate the globe often report hallucinations involving friends with whom they believed they were conversing. Many of these brave sailors carry tapes to listen to, they record their voices as if they were speaking to others, and when-

ever possible they establish radio contact with operators ashore—
if only to chat.

Yet in the midst of a wealth of human beings, Pattern Preservers
often live in virtual isolation, clinging tenaciously to the small, customary group of friends, with little or no interest in reaching out.
Pattern Breakers, on the other hand, are always wide open to the
formation of new friendships; in fact for them the motivating force
behind breaking patterns is the desire to set new people-patterns.
They know that in addition to the enjoyment, they gain the major
portion of their knowledge from the people they meet, and they
aren't going to allow this education to come to a standstill. Also,
they've learned through experience that to relate successfully with
people, they can't think in terms of an activity that can be picked up
and set down at one's convenience. Instead, meaningful relating
must be an ongoing theme that lies at the heart of everything they do.

The individual who is cautious about forming friendships quite
often ends up with very few or no friends. On the other hand,
people with open minds and emotions can find something in common with everyone they meet, and many of the most casual
encounters turn into firm friendships. These attitudes can only be
described as admittedly and unabashedly naive, and it isn't surprising that Pattern Breakers are often targets for criticism or
recipients of well-intentioned warnings that they should be careful about "getting close" to this or that person. But through-and-
through Pattern Breakers are never careful about closeness; they
know that some of their most fantastic relationships have come
from times when they've thrown caution to the winds.

A rule of thumb that Tom and I have developed for setting people-patterns is that, generally speaking, every person we meet *is*
what he or she *is to us*. In the midst of a mode that basically has no
walls—we sleep with open hatches and conduct our activities in
the open environment of bays and marinas—a great many individuals, of diverse origins and personalities, are constantly passing through our lives. In our experience these people will nearly
always deliver what is expected of them, the exceptions being so
few that it would be foolish to change our practices because of

them. On the other hand, those persons we have known who have expected trouble from the people they meet have unfailingly projected that negative stance and have nearly always gotten exactly what they expected.

A few years back, an open approach to an unusual person we had met paid off in a dramatic way; a stage play couldn't have been more dramatically illustrative of the wisdom of freely handing out friendship. On a small Caribbean island we had made close friends with Albert, who had been born to a fisherman's family in Dominica. He was making his way "by hook or by crook," doing odd jobs on boats and was, we gathered, always teetering on the brink of being sent back home, for lack of proper papers. We pursued Albert's acquaintance amid a chorus of gloomy warnings that boiled down to, "he's out for what he can get from you," never catching the slightest glimpse of any negative qualities. On the contrary Albert always insisted on giving more than he had received, appearing beside the boat with three cold drinks he had just purchased from the marina store—when our icebox was jammed with a dozen of the same—with fresh fruit he had bought for us in the open market, or—because he knew I liked flowers— an armful of poinciana or some other variety of tropical blooms. In addition he seemed to spring out of nowhere whenever we were bogged down in some difficult boat chore. The real vindication of our trust in Albert—the "stage production" that stilled for all times the voices of our cautious friends—took place shortly before his inevitable deportation.

Romany Star and crew were arriving on a super-gusty day to a slip in a marina that is notorious for its oily, dirty water. Just as we were ready to make our final turn into a space, through a mess of drifting garbage and murk, we were horrified to hear our motor give the unhealthy splutter and terminal sigh that always signalled the recurrence of a long-term problem we had been having. Engineless, Romany Star began drifting backward toward the rusted, jagged bowsprit of a nearby fishing vessel, and there was neither time nor space to throw an anchor. Albert, who was hanging off the edge of a waiting group of our friends on the dock, realized our straits and promptly plunged, fully clothed, into the filthy water, caught our bowline and swam it to the nearest piling. Later, after he had taken a thorough shower and was sipping a cool drink in our cockpit, his former detractors sat in friendly fashion alongside him, doling out praise to the person they had formerly despised, and bringing to a happy ending a real-life play that was reminiscent of the moralistic scripts of silent movie days.

An open attitude toward people, coupled with a genuine curiosity about what they're doing, pays off in many ways—some of them monetary. Two of the most enthusiastic Pattern Breakers we know are an eightyish couple we first met several decades ago when we stopped for gas at a small service station in Maryland. Seeing our out-of-state license tag, Paul and Ava struck up a conversation with us, wanting to know all about where we were from and where we were going, and proceeded to treat us to a complimentary glass of cold apple cider. On the basis of that gesture and the accompanying conversation, a hard and fast friendship was formed. We weren't the only people so favored, however. These two delighted in getting to know scores of new individuals every day of their lives, and the effects on their business were almost more than they could handle. Today they own a large service center, with several employees, in the same location, and on our last visit we could see that they were still as fascinated with the passing stream of Americana as they ever were. With no financial reason to keep on working, they're at it as energetically as ever, and they look and act at least fifteen years younger than their chronological ages.

Just as Paul and Ava are traveling all over the country while staying put, by vicariously sharing the experiences of their customers, it is also possible to travel all over the world and never leave one's hometown. Foreign students at universities and colleges are always eager to make friends, and when they are invited for dinner, they bring with them a wealth of information that they are longing to share. Language is no barrier, since in order to be able to study, they must have a fair knowledge of English. Parents and children alike can learn much from these students, but if the family-rearing days are over, there is still good reason to explore the world in this way. Student exchange programs, which bring young people from overseas right into your home to live, also provide interesting situations.

Adherence to social strata is a major inhibitor in making friends. Pattern Preservers wouldn't dream of forming close relationships with people beneath their social level, but Pattern Breakers make a point of penetrating those barriers. Volunteer welfare work is one good way of making meaningful contact. Al, a ham radio friend of ours, has become active in the Big Brother program in his area. Jimmy, the young man he spends time with on a weekly basis and to whom he is always available by phone, comes from an impoverished family that is minus a male figure. Al's conversation is full of their experiences together, and one senses that he is reaping at least as many benefits as is his young charge. This interest has recently expanded into the formation of a softball team for a group of boys such as Jimmy, with Al and some of his ham friends serving as coaches. Al's wife, through what has become a close family relationship with Jimmy, is now involved with the other children in the family and is giving the mother a helping hand, with used clothing collected from friends, transportation to the doctor, advice on various problems. Some of the problems encountered by this struggling group are real eye-openers for people who have been born and reared on a more privileged level. And this lifelong isolation in a social stratum is certainly a pattern that should be broken.

Entrance into the sphere of the very wealthy and powerful can also be instructive, but owing to the barriers erected by money, this kind of experience is not always easy to come by. One way to gain entrance to this interesting area is through employment. A woman we know who found herself in need of a job after a divorce decided she would like to put her homemaking talents to use. She became a housekeeper for one of America's "oldest" families. Although her background had been quite comfortable, the experiences she had in this household, where people she had read about in the newspapers were daily visitors, were a constant source of interest. Many years ago I enjoyed a similar adventure, working for one week as a tutor in a household that ranked near the top in the annals of our country's financial empire. My assignment was to teach a grandchild who had been flown to Miami in order to recuperate from an operation. It was amusing to suddenly become one of a staff of housekeeper, chauffeur, cooks, and maids and gardeners galore, plus numerous other personnel such as beauticians and masseurs, who made regular visits. My "rank" was high enough to rate being waited on, so my young student and I enjoyed elegantly served refreshments and luncheons beside the pool. The experience was an education in how well some people can afford to live, and how alike all humanity is at the core; also—very important at that particular time in our family's history—the pay was incredibly good.

Middle-class Pattern Preservers would most certainly frown on programmed entrance into the environs of legendary wealth and power, but Pattern Breakers refuse to close their minds to experiencing the full gamut of life. Pattern Breakers feel that all people are equally deserving of attention, interest, and interrelating—all the way from the very poor to the very rich. They know the difference between mere curiosity and an honest desire to form relationships. And they refuse to follow the example of those who never try to form friendships with anyone who is at either of the extreme ends of the economic spectrum.

Mutual need is one of the most common pivots around which friendships are developed, and although we have the same emotional requirement today for association that humans have always had, the easy fulfillment of our daily needs has alienated us from one another. As a result, setting new people-patterns can take place right in one's neighborhood. The field is fertile because, regrettably, communities of the type that formerly thrived on helping each other are today groupings of walled fortresses, and few residents get to know one another. Automobiles slide in and out of automatically opened and closed doors, and except for times when the grass needs mowing or the mail has to be brought in, figures are seldom seen outside. Since nearly everyone in today's society has transportation, and since stores are open till late at night, there's no more need to borrow a cup of sugar or a bit of salt. Furthermore, the coffee klatch and evening get-togethers have been virtually wiped out by ready entertainment on television. Adding to the problem . . . the days of spacious front porches with swings and comfortable chairs, where neighbors congregated to keep cool on warm summer evenings, have come to an end with the advent of air conditioning, and few residences are built nowadays with anything more than a token porch. The message that people don't need people anymore is loud and clear, but Pattern Breakers aren't listening. On the contrary they never cease to let people know that they need them. And they aren't shy about taking the first step.

Kathleen moved into a typically cold neighborhood and decided right off that she would do something about it. She took on a big task, because this rather affluent community didn't even have the uniting influence of small children; the young people who lived there were of college age, deriving their social contact from their campuses. Kathleen began meeting everyone, paying the old-fashioned kind of social call—usually carrying a plate of homemade candy or cookies. After this initial step she started a series of small gatherings of several families at her home. As others became interested, block parties were organized, then larger outdoor affairs that included the entire neighborhood. Soon people were jogging or walking in groups; flower enthusiasts could be seen carrying bouquets to those who were under the weather; over-the-fence conversations were a common sight. Part of the pleasure in arriving home was the exchanging of pleasantries around the mailboxes.

The fringe benefits of getting to know one another soon surfaced. It was convenient, everyone discovered, to have a list of names and numbers for those times when someone was needed to keep an eye on the dog or cat or to water the plants . . . or when a wife, left alone at night, heard a suspicious noise . . . or when vacationers remembered they'd left the basement door unlocked. Also, the difficult times—such as when family members became ill—or the times to be celebrated—when someone graduated from college or got married—were all shared now. Experience laid to rest those nagging fears that getting close to people would result in having one's house constantly mobbed by them. And the whole beautiful thing happened because a Pattern Breaker took the first step.

The unabashed naïveté of Pattern Breakers often leads them to take the first step in getting to know people. After making so many great friends in this way, they become afraid *not* to make the first move, since a truly fantastic relationship might be missed. And if the person turns out to be a stiff-backed Pattern Preserver, the rebuff doesn't leave any wounds whatsoever. Jewels can turn up at the most unexpected times. One day a dark-haired lady in a cool, flower-printed dress came strolling down the dock, then paused for a moment in front of Romany Star, apparently studying our boat's design. From my seat in the cockpit I called out a "hello" and proceeded to invite her aboard to check out the interior. She and her husband, who were visiting the British Virgins from New Mexico, returned that evening for drinks; we discovered a long list of common interests, and the ground was laid for a friendship that has gone full force for several years. This "first hello" technique has become the pattern for many friendships, and Romany Star's guest book is jammed with names and addresses of people met in this casual way.

Late one afternoon in a bay off St. John's Island in the U.S. Virgins, Tom and I dinghied up to a charter boat that had just dropped anchor close to us. The three couples lounging in the cockpit invited us aboard for a cool drink and during the subsequent conversation revealed that they had hoped to dine that evening at an elegant restaurant on shore, but had discovered that one of the men had failed to bring the required jacket and tie. Tom solved this crisis by fetching these items from Romany Star's hanging locker, and we spent the next day swimming and snorkeling together and finding out more about each other. These people, too, have become dear friends, and regular correspondence keeps us all up to date on each other's activities.

One of our most interesting friendships arose from a bus stop encounter. In Marigot, St. Martin, we spotted a young woman sitting on a wall that bordered the sidewalk and asked if she knew when the next bus was due to arrive. We soon found out that she was from Paris, born of Italian parents who had migrated to France, and a humorous session ensued, based on what we knew of Spanish and French and on her knowledge of Italian (closely related to Spanish) and French. As we rode together on the bus, she issued an invitation to her home. And in the ensuing weeks we shared many delightful visits with this young couple, who were employed in the local construction business. They enjoyed Sunday sailing trips on Romany Star, and we benefited from evenings spent in a French atmosphere in which we were forced to improve our knowledge of the language, since no one but us knew more than two or three words of English.

Setting new people-patterns takes time, but Pattern Breakers are likely to let all but the most urgent chores wait until tomorrow when there's a chance to make new friendships—or simply to chat with people they've known for a long time. Ham radio operators are masters of the art of giving time to conversing. And listening to their patter, important or purely inconsequential, one cannot help but sense that this is what life is meant to be—a hooking up of minds and personalities . . . the finding of common interests . . . the simple pleasure of communication. On the other hand, Pattern Preservers give their attention to only the narrow area of subject matter and people that they have decided is worth their time, walking through their lives with earmuffs and blinders on, choosing not to connect with the vast wealth of experience that lies outside their chosen zone. The man who played golf in Spain and saw nothing different from his club course back home was absolutely right: a golf course is a golf course wherever it may be, with variations in layout, climate, and vegetation, but with the same offered goal—to drive the ball successfully from hole to hole. The real difference to be found in playing golf in Spain or in Florida lies entirely with the people. People are the receivers and transmitters of almost everything that's worth learning . . . and are all—rich or poor, bright or dull, morally upright or corrupt—worth getting to know.

The sage who said, "As long as you are interested in people, you'll never be bored," was dispensing the prescription for breaking patterns when neither time nor money is available for travel, but a willingness does exist to cast inhibitions aside and spend time truly getting to know persons who may have been friends or acquaintances for years. With a little prompting, most people love talking about themselves, since they seldom have the opportunity to do so. Back in the days when Tom and I were knee-deep in the "nesting" phase, and still had not joined the ranks of bona fide Pattern Breakers, we learned a people-pattern lesson that has affected our whole approach to establishing relationships. Our teachers were a cheerful-looking couple in their early seventies who lived next door.

Mabel and I often chatted for a few moments over the backyard fence and sometimes borrowed cooking ingredients from each other, but I'm ashamed to admit that in a two-year period of living side by side, we had never sat down for an in-depth conversation. One day our eldest son broke an arm, and since Tom was at work with our only car, the always-friendly couple next door offered a ride to the nearest hospital. As the doctor attended to the patient, the three of us had time for our first real talk, and—perhaps to show me that adversity doesn't have to get one down—they revealed some stunning facts about their background. I knew that Mabel and Herb (legally adopted names) were of Jewish extraction, born, respectively, in Germany and Russia, but little had I suspected that this always-smiling woman had witnessed the shooting and mass-grave burial of her parents and all her brothers and sisters. She had barely escaped death by melting into the ranks of some Gentile friends, who sheltered her until the Allied occupation. In later get-togethers we learned that Herb had worked for the railway system in Russia, and he was full of stories of how the equipment was patched together and the trains kept running through sheer ingenuity, in the absence of the appropriate technology. We were living next door to a treasure of experiences, courage, and wisdom and had only accidentally made the gut-level connection.

Whereas Pattern Preservers are instantly turned off by situations that don't click with their private world of experience, Pattern Breakers are always on the lookout for unusual backgrounds and philosophies. For them diversity is a uniting factor. Although they're also always interested in people with their own background (after all, no two people are identical), they are ready to listen to the expounding of any belief that doesn't downgrade human rights, no matter how "far out." Maintaining an open mind and respecting the opinions, customs, and personalities of others go hand in hand. One of our dearest friends—a man we met in Guadeloupe—is of a decidedly militant nature, travels with a full arsenal of guns, swords, and just about every hostile piece of machinery available that can be stowed on a boat. He has never had to use these wicked items, but it is clear that he not only feels properly defended at all times but also, for some curious reason, derives enjoyment from the possession of his ugly collection. Tom and I possess not one weapon, even though we sometimes travel in areas of questionable security, since our preference, foolish or wise, is not to bear arms. Our position and thoughts and the opposing ones of our friend have been made clear, and the subject has been filed for all time. To people who know us there seems to be no common ground for uniting these personalities that appear to be at opposite poles, but in actuality there are many areas of shared interests, among them languages, love of animals, travel. We are in contact with what are to us the agreeable facets of a complex personality. If we rejected this man because of his militant (in the name of self-defense) approach to life, we would miss out on all those areas of experience and knowledge that have provided us with so much pleasure.

Unusual people can be found in the most unexpected places. Probably the most incongruous friendship find of our lives has been a recommended Buddhist monk who has settled on a mountain in the southeastern states. We met him quite accidentally and enjoyed his company so much that we would drive many miles out of our way just to drop by for a brief chat. He has taught us a lot: the value of pure water; surprising methods for gardening, which do not include the customary neat rows but involve clumps of different vegetables. He's taught us that with the proper food and exercise the human body can stay beautiful and strong until a very advanced chronological age; that a person can be harmoniously happy within a simple existence; that it is possible to be a purely open channel to relating with anyone alive, although cultures are worlds apart. He has scores of close friends on this foreign soil—certain proof that diversity can be one of the most unifying of factors.

Anything less than a comfortable attitude toward diversity would have nipped in the bud our friendship with another French family in Marigot. The very first visit they paid to our boat, on a drowsy Sunday afternoon in Marigot Bay, was the scene of an event that fell somewhat short of coinciding with our usual way of doing things. During the delightful evening we had spent ashore with them two days before, it had been clear that the teenage son and daughter were being brought up in a family atmosphere that rivaled the prototypical Stateside home; in fact I had attached a "decidedly conservative" mental tag to our new friends. Aboard Romany Star, after a luncheon I served on trays in the cockpit, the conversation continued for an hour or so, till we all decided that it was time to take a nap or go for a swim. Everyone was attired in bathing suits, so all we had to do was to get the energy to dive overboard. At this point the mother stood up, nonchalantly peeled off her bathing suit top, stretched, then dove overboard. Her teenage daughter, imitating her in every detail, did the same, leaving me to declare my inhibitions by swimming in complete bathing attire. Later, drying off together in the cockpit, with fastening of tops being done by father and son—in the presence of Tom's carefully averted eyes, our lesson in how some people from France prefer to swim was concluded. And to be truthful there was nothing to criticize; the whole affair was their natural way of doing things.

The process of breaking people-patterns goes hand in hand with setting new ones. Though a great deal of emotional support can be gained on both sides from long-standing relationships, there comes a time in many friendships when constant exposure to each other curtails personal growth. A Pattern Breaker's head-on crash into the wall of a Preserver's stubborn ways is often a reliable signal that greener friendship pastures lie elsewhere . . . at least, in terms of regular activities together. To use the old cliché, some of our best friends are Pattern Preservers. Their loyalty is beyond question, and there is a strong mutual affection, but our minds and desires have taken off in a direction that doesn't foster long periods of time spent together in an ambience that is happy for all. Human beings develop differently, and the fact of life is that the most enjoyable friendships grow from some field of shared interest.

By the same token, many relationships have, from the very outset, so little basis for development that a polite termination of time spent together—though not of the total association—is the best solution. Although all people are worth getting to know, when one person's mind is consistently channeled in a direction that is decidedly disagreeable to the other person, the possibility of mutual growth just doesn't exist. The effective setting of people-patterns allows the freedom to politely detach oneself from dedicating time and effort to situations that aren't going anywhere. And everyone will be better off for the decision.

A widow with whom we spent a great deal of time before our recommencement provides a good illustration. Our interest link had been with her husband, but after his death we naturally wanted to keep in close touch with her. Everything about this woman's personality was contrary to what we enjoyed, and evenings spent with her could progress only on the basis of our agreeing with her approach to life—a personality bent she had exhibited since our very first meeting. The sole common ground after her husband's demise was our desire to comfort her and her desire to be comforted. After a year of painful weekly dinners with her, we decided, with a great deal of accompanying guilt, to see her only on a limited basis and proceeded to give her weekly excuses that were carefully calculated not to hurt her feelings. Not surprisingly, without our hovering influence, she launched out on a series of activities that brought her a lot of happiness—all without the help or advice of the pair of Good Samaritans who thought she couldn't make it without their constant company.

It is always refreshing to break people-patterns with obnoxious, know-it-all types, the social boors who never hear what anyone else has to say. In these one-sided situations there is little taking place, and to continue dedicating time to listening to them is to feed their addiction to the sound of their own voice. I recall a long-suffering relationship with a man of this ilk, who delighted in insulting everyone in his environs: his hosts' stereo wasn't up to par . . . the food could do with a bit more of this or that . . . the balcony wall obstructed the view . . . in short, nothing outside his own home was ever right. In this case the wife was such a nice person that it seemed wrong to break off our relationship with them. However, when we began breaking patterns, in the days just prior to our recommencement, the final blow was struck, and the boor was given the opportunity to shape up or ship out. Ray owned a wooden boat and spent a great deal of money to keep it in polished condition. We were constantly praising his vessel, for she is a fine ship, but upon buying Romany Star, we noticed that compliments for our wood-trimmed fiberglass craft were noticeably absent. One day, on a visit to our beloved future home, Ray declared in a loud voice, "Well, I'm going to see if there are any good-looking wooden boats in the marina. All I've seen so far are nothing but Tupperware!" To put it succinctly, that did it. We didn't say anything, because an argument was not what we desired; instead we lapsed into an icy silence that provided Ray the opportunity to apologize. No apology forthcoming, our continued pointed silence brought the occasion, and for all effects, the relationship, to an end. We both managed to give Ray's poor little wife a friendly arm squeeze as they trooped off the boat. We have never felt any regrets over breaking that pattern, and I'm sure that Ray hasn't felt any either. One can only hope that his wife is a privileged participant in some marvelous hidden side of his nature that makes it all worthwhile.

Although the easiest way to break people-patterns is by moving away, Pattern Breakers sometimes find that a geographical solution is outside the realm of their possibilities. Fortunately for them the very act of breaking patterns automatically shifts their lives over to a new set of friends and, in the best of outcomes, to richer vistas for people—on every side of the change—who were mired in unfruitful associations. An important phase of these new attachments is the help that individuals who have "been there" can provide. Pattern Breakers who have decided to build an unusual kind of house, or a house in an unusual place, are better off to avail themselves of the experience of anyone who has ever done the same. Experience is the best and most expensive teacher, and pioneers in any field are always happy to talk about the mistakes they've made in order to finally achieve success. The man who decides to hire only ex-convicts as employees will have experiences to share with others who follow this worthwhile route . . . the small business adventurer has learned a lot along the way . . . students are the best guides to settling down on campus . . . people who have gone into the creative arts are nearly always ready to give advice to the struggling novice . . . Recommencers who decide to run motels or small hotels can escape many pitfalls by consulting with veterans of the business.

Anyone who travels for very long finds out that tourist brochures often omit important data, especially if the data are of a negative nature. People's health or lives have been saved by checking with other travelers as to the presence of bilharzia (a damaging microorganism) in tropical rivers or poisonous fruits and plants, such as the delicious-looking and equally deadly manchineel apple, which grows in many tropical areas. Even the rainwater dripping from a manchineel tree can be harmful to the skin. A stellar example of people helping people is found in the Seven Seas Cruising Association's monthly bulletin (500 S.E. 17th Street, Suite 220, Fort Lauderdale, Fla. 33316), an inexpensive publication that is available to anyone interested enough in boating to want to be a subscriber. The content consists entirely of letters from the many live-aboard commodores, as well as from associate members who cruise from time to time. Voyagers can check out the personal experiences of others before making their own trips, with topics including attitudes of local governments, customs that should be respected, availability and cost of food and medical supplies, sailing hazards in the vicinity, sights that shouldn't be missed, information on anchorages, and some riveting descriptions of sailing adventures. Long before we even dreamed of living on a boat, Tom and I found vicarious pleasure in reading the SSCA bulletins.

For land travelers, "inside information" issued on a regular basis by NEAR and IAMAT (fully discussed in "Patterns for Good Health") includes many items that are not related to health and that resemble in some respects the thrust of the SSCA material. And of course the reader-input sections and most of the articles in the various travel magazines provide another way of getting help from people who have "been there."

Breaking people-patterns and setting new ones is one of the very best ways to stay young. Youth is, after all, a state of change and vitality, and few things put a more effective damper on vitality than do monotonous personal relationships. It would be hard, perhaps impossible, to find any chronologically older person who has managed to stay young who is not consistently involved in setting new people-patterns. In this respect the mother of a friend of ours provides a good example. A heavy source of concern to her pattern-preserving offspring, she refuses, even as an octogenarian, to stay put and let her family give her the "proper care." If she can't be traveling in some interesting, faraway spot, she will set out in her own city, striking up on-the-spot friendships with everyone she meets—taxi drivers, bus drivers, sales people, waitresses—and is not beyond sending a birthday card to someone she sits beside on the Staten Island ferry. Young and old are recipients of her attention, but she is quite discriminatory about her doctors; they have to be at least seventy years old. She feels it takes that long to get a good grasp on medicine. She is still going strong, managing to drive her relatives to distraction with long periods of communication blackouts, when she forgets to write from Timbuktu or nearby Denver. But when you see her in a family gathering with all the worriers, she is younger than anyone present.

This vivacious octogenarian Pattern Breaker found out a long time ago that the biggest adventure going consisted of breaking and setting people-patterns. To discoverers of this truth, age considerations fly out of the window when making friends. They would never be guilty of joining associations for the elderly for any other reason than that there was some interesting activity going on that they wanted to be a part of. They are just as likely to be found having fun with a group of young people as sitting with other senior citizens at a bingo party, because they usually manage to keep fit enough for anything they want to do. They have found out that the chronologically young always have time for anyone who is genuinely interested in their lives, and they realize that the chronologically older have played a heavy role in carving the generation gap, by consistently segregating their activities and attention—to the detriment of everyone concerned.

In our five years of living and cruising aboard Romany Star, people have been the biggest adventure of all. The sights have been memorable, for who could forget a full, white moon turning night into day on the wide expanse of shoreless sea, the sunsets and sunrises viewed on the water's horizon, or, after a long trip, the sight of green mountains jutting suddenly out of a deep blue ocean. But it has been the people who have given us the best experiences of all—the ones we're always talking about.

A relationship we'll never forget was formed in the town of Fort de France on the island of Martinique, and was ended, probably forever, after a period of four hours. At that point in our cruising life our knowledge of French was at its sparsest level—virtually limited to *bonjour* and *au revoir*—so it was with a good deal of hesitation that we approached a well-dressed, straw-hatted gentleman on the street bordering the city pier, to inquire as to the time. We pointed to his wristwatch and he smilingly showed us the dial, then proceeded with a rattling of French to tow us into the nearest cafe for a cold glass of juice. His rapid-fire speech wiped out our small possibility for understanding, but as he hurried us from cafe to bakery to bar to another cafe, we had the most wonderfully nonsensical time—laughing a lot, making gestures and pointing, but never establishing a single sentence of meaningful communication. As the afternoon progressed, no one wanted to end the zany revelry and on we went, as he chattered a mile a minute, trekking up and down the narrow streets of historic old Fort de France with periodic pauses for refreshment.

Our new-found friend seemed to have understood that we were boating people, from the dockside area where we had met and from a sailboat pendant I had shown him in trying to illustrate our origins. After four hours of incoherent fun together, having reached an impressive level of human understanding without the benefit of language, he steered us back down to the dock and stood smiling as we lowered ourselves into our dinghy. We pointed toward our boat, anchored in the distant outer fringes of the bay, in mute invitation to join us—unable to convey that we were sailing away the next morning—but he tapped his watch and shook his head. I made writing gestures, seeking pen and paper for exchanging addresses, but he answered with a regretful "*non*." We managed "*au revoir*," and he responded with a heavily accented "good-bye," then reached in his pocket and extracted a beautiful key chain, stripped off the keys, and pressed it into my hand. As we motored out, leaving behind a wonderful four-hour friendship, we realized that we hadn't even been able to understand his name. Still, something about that crazy afternoon, when words hadn't really been necessary and nothing but the desire to be together had carried us along, has made that anonymous Frenchman stand out among the many people we've met since entering our pattern-breaking life-style.

S E T T I N G   N E W
M A R R I A G E
P A T T E R N S

In the days before we became Pattern Breakers, our marriage framework followed lines that were characteristic of that era. Tom was the acknowledged breadwinner, and I was the housewife and mother who made occasional stabs at having a career as teacher and/or writer. Our activities were largely centered around our home and children and included some good times with a reasonably varied circle of friends. Looking back, I believe the four of us were quite satisfied with the way we lived. Even in those days we managed to involve ourselves in enough stimulating diversion to stave off boredom, and for the long haul of those child-rearing years, I found it enormously appealing to live within a framework wherein the strong male figure protects and provides for the nest while the mother hen concentrates on all those warm, housewifely tasks. Indeed, is there anything more gladdening than a house that has just been polished up to a nice shine and in which a hot meal is in the oven, children are bathed and pajamaed and playing happily on the living room rug, the mother is showered and perfumed, and a grateful father comes bursting through the front door? For us life was sweet enough.

For all the positive aspects, however, there was an inexorable flaw in that happy little scene: the time arrived when two of the leading characters had grown up and moved away from home, and the two who were left behind had to either settle for surviving on old memories and getting their major jollies out of the "young folks'" activities or to opt for grabbing their precious freedom and running with it into a life so vibrant that everyone, offspring included, could only benefit from the transformation. In fact, next in line to the top winners in pattern-breaking adventures are those everwatchful sons and daughters. There are few better gifts to one's children than to set the example of new marriage patterns that will defy all the traditionally stagnant molds. On the other hand, there are few things more demoralizing to children than the sight of their parents' degeneration into inactivity—a heavy signal as to their own destiny when they reach the same stage in life.

For full-time Pattern Breakers new marriage patterns are a natural consequence of what they're doing. The old, familiar roles either fall completely by the wayside or undergo a radical and decidedly salutary revamping, with some interesting—and totally unanticipated—personality changes and new roles emerging. These changes take place because activities strongly influence the features of one's personality. Happily, as Pattern Breakers change in their new and challenging lives, the personalities that enter the marriage framework are more complete and far stronger—a situation that brings about some startling benefits in every important area of the relationship. All these bonuses are lost, however, if both partners do not go wholeheartedly into the new life-style; the resultant pressures can endanger or destroy a marriage.

Since total involvement by husband and wife is a vital ingredient for success, it is important that in the new venture, both partners be as equal as is possible in know-how and overall responsibility. The more involved a person becomes in the different facets of an experience, the more interested he or she will be in the undertaking as a whole, while if one partner is simply "brought along," with few or no important duties, trouble is sure to ensue. Based on our own experiences it's clear that if a woman were assigned solely to the cleaning and cooking chores on a boat, it wouldn't take her long to decide that she would be far better off keeping house on land, since a boat is not a proper house—no matter how comfortable (for one thing, it is in constant motion, even at dock). On the other hand, if she is there for tasks as important as the man's, in relation to the major goal—to move the boat successfully from port to port—the housekeeping part can be enjoyable. All the cleanliness and comfort she is bringing about is adding to the total mutual experience. The principles involved in the boating context would apply in almost any new pattern.

None of this means, however, that old skills and interests have to be abandoned in a mutual endeavor. Whereas I enjoy taking command of the aesthetic features of the boat's interior, Tom is more drawn to the mechanical side—the motors for Romany Star and her dinghy, the pumps—and the electrical system. Nevertheless, he has learned to cook since moving aboard, can clean as well as I can, and often shares in those chores, while I participate in some way in most repairs—holding the wrench for stubborn nuts and screws, handing over tools, consulting on possible causes of breakdowns, and just being there with sympathy when things don't go right . . . as is often the case on boats. But the true metamorphosis in our marriage setup takes place when we are sailing. At this time our husband and wife relationship virtually disappears; whoever is at the tiller is captain at that moment. We are simply two people working together with the common goal of making the trip as smooth as possible. Tom is better at steering for long periods of time in heavy seas because he is physically stronger. I'm better at docking the boat because I seem to have a more sensitive touch for handling Romany Star in small spaces. We have equal knowledge of sailing practices and navigation procedures (dead reckoning and celestial), and since we're doing our pattern breaking at sea, this equal ability makes sense for safety, too; if one were incapacitated, the other could bring in the boat singlehandedly.

A short time after we had started sailing together on our own little racing sloop, our two sons, who had been away from home for a while, had their first opportunity to see their parents' new relationship. They still hadn't learned to sail so were on this trip as spectators. We took them out into an area that can become quite choppy, and in the process had to shout some rather strong commands and replies. After the sea had calmed down a bit and we could both relax and enjoy some family conversation, we turned to look for the first time at our passengers, who had been silent throughout our sailing exercise. Their faces were decidedly serious, and since both loved the water and had surfed and disported in it for many years, I couldn't believe that what I was seeing was fear.

"What's the matter?" their father inquired. "Don't you like sailing?"

"We like sailing," Larry replied tersely.

"Yeah," Tom Jr. added, "but we've never seen you two guys acting like that around each other."

Tom and I broke down in laughter, and our sons soon joined in. They had seen their parents' "sailor-to-sailor" personalities for the first time, and after the initial shock they were beginning to like the whole idea.

The couples we have known who have been successful at RV-ing, farming, living on foreign soil, or breaking patterns on familiar ground have unfailingly been those who have "caught the flame" with equal fervor and have become equally involved in the endeavor. Denise has been married for thirty years to a welfare worker who is a committed social reformer, having dedicated his life to worthy—and often unpopular—causes. Jack is a personable and intelligent man, of impressive educational background, and could have gone to the top in any profession he might have chosen. Instead the family has always lived on a limited budget and at one time spent a long and difficult period of time on special assignment to a sadly deprived area. Denise does the typing and editing of Jack's newspaper submissions, provides constructive critical input for all his projects, helps him with community meetings, and in truth is his right arm. If she had been less involved than Jack in their goal, either the marriage or the mission would surely have fallen to pieces long ago. The flak he has often taken from the media and the people around them would in itself have dealt the final blow. Fortunately, though, both are equally enthusiastic. They've reared some outstanding children, and the marriage framework of this admirable pair has felt all the benefits that day-to-day pattern breaking can provide.

When RV-ing across the country, both partners—in the ideal situation—should share the driving and campground chores. Although the wife usually attends to the inside tasks while her husband takes care of the business arrangements and the electrical and water connections, both should know how to do everything. On the highway the fact that the rig is heavy and delicate to handle shouldn't bar the woman from the wheel of a modern vehicle; just sitting and looking at the scenery can get boring. Friends of ours who have been successful at this kind of pattern breaking have shared all jobs. The same goes for any new pattern—for example, farming, building an unusual type of house, living the lives of full-time students, traveling or residing in foreign countries, or forming relationships with people from a wide variety of social and economic backgrounds. The wife who drives a lot of nails and paints a lot of walls in her new house and the husband who helps plan color schemes and shares in the chore of tracking down wallpaper and fabrics are going to share more completely in the successes and the inevitable mistakes and hence are going to feel more a part of the total project.

In the traditional marriage, roles are so stereotyped that much of the interaction is simply a replay of what has been witnessed, leaving little room for originality. The sad part of all this mimicry is that qualities and talents can be hidden forever, since there is no impetus for divulging them. Pattern Breakers, however, find themselves in situations where every capability is constantly being dredged out and used. Since events are full of surprise, one must always rise to the occasion, and in order to cope with the unexpected, undreamed-of abilities come to light. As a person who was terrified of the water, being a full-time sailor was the remotest thought I could have entertained. Not as dramatic, but quite surprising, has been the fact that I find mechanics to be an interesting field. Though not as absorbed in the subject as Tom, I enjoy helping him as he searches for the mysterious source of a leak or the cause of a slow engine start-up. My interests have surely been sharpened by such happenings as the appearance of too much water in the bilge when land was nowhere in sight or by an engine failure just at the moment when we were out of wind and only a few miles away from our evening anchorage.

Friends of ours who settled in southern Spain were surprised to find that they both enjoyed learning Spanish; the wife had been delegated to handle language chores on all the short trips they took, but when everyday necessity pointed out the need for communication, the husband actually turned out to be more facile than she in mastering the puzzles of conjugation and agreement. Another couple who adopted two emotionally deprived, undernourished children, ages eight and ten, have found some unsuspected talents for meeting their charges' needs. The husband, who had thought of his wife as being the leader in the undertaking, has found that his abilities are equally needed, and that in many cases the techniques he has devised for meeting the daily crises have been the most effective.

The man and woman who launch a new pattern-breaking life together find that one of the biggest benefits to their marriage is the fact that they become more interesting to each other. This is the natural result of being involved in challenging situations. As the new circumstances summon forth new abilities and personality facets, a more spirited person evolves, and the spouse is on the scene to witness the transformation. Married people who are bored with each other usually fail to realize that it's their monotonous routine that is largely at fault; an exciting state of affairs can work wonders on the dullest personality. Enid and Bob, married in their late teens, and now in their mid-forties, had a run-of-the-mill marriage until Bob was transferred to his company's branch in San Juan, Puerto Rico. Their children were grown and away from home, and before the overseas transfer Bob spent most of his free time playing golf, while his bored wife tried to keep busy with garden club meetings and bridge get-togethers. Boredom has been called the Number One Enemy of marriage, and although these two were not yet headed for the divorce courts, their relationship had definitely lost its glow. In San Juan both were required by the husband's employer to study Spanish, and they began to have some hilarious times practicing the day's lesson with each other every evening. Enid showed a knack for dealing with the household inconveniences and shopping hassles that are common outside the continental United States, and Bob proved adept at conducting business under circumstances that were considerably more challenging than those back home. Amid all this excitement their personalities began to sparkle, a glow settled over their marriage, and a totally unexpected Pattern Breaker came into their lives—a baby. Though this kind of challenge is not for everyone, it has done wonders for Enid and Bob, and certainly no one can accuse them of living humdrum lives.

It is no accident that Pattern Breakers' personalities sparkle. Just as the average couple on a great vacation are full of life, relaxed, and spilling over with jokes and laughter—as opposed to their more subdued behavior back on those jobs they aren't really wild about—so Pattern Breakers, who are busy with what they enjoy doing, be it hard or easy, consistently display that agreeable "vacation personality." And marrieds who are that happy about life can't help but feel those good reverberations in every corner of their relationship.

When both partners are enthusiastically pulling together in a new life-style, the logical result is a stronger relationship. A marriage usually consists of a series of joint efforts—the establishing of a home, the rearing of a family, the establishing of retirement life—as well as gaps in activity, such as the period after the children have left home or when retirement is in full swing but nothing's happening. Those gaps, when no communicating is going on about what to do about Jane's allergies or where to send James Jr. to college, are the points at which the relationship is in danger of weakening. But how different the picture is for Pattern Breakers! If the new life mode is as thrilling as it should be, communication is on the highest level ever. Gone are the divisive elements that plagued the old days, when the husband was growing and developing in his job and the wife, unless endowed with a remarkable personal philosophy, was having difficulty keeping some degree of sanity while concentrating on cleaning bathrooms and vacuuming rugs. But here to stay, for Pattern Breakers, are the uniting forces of working together in a visible, down-to-earth way, for a common goal. It's hard to relate the details of cleaning bathrooms to the fact of being on a husband-wife team that is overcoming the problems of life, but it's oh so easy to relate struggling together with a foreign language in a food market overseas to the pleasure of eating the delicious dinner for two that results from all that exertion, or to relate the joint effort of opening house and heart for flocks of foreign students to the warm feelings that emerge on all sides. For the physically adventuresome who hang-glide, mountain climb, or take the long hike along the Appalachian Trail, there's the shared and uniting thrill of triumphing over the inherent risks. A great outcome of all this is that as husband and wife share the successes of breaking the language barrier abroad or of making foreign students feel at home or in enjoying a physical adventure, they are at the same time becoming stronger individually and more united.

Pattern-breaking husbands and wives refuse to fall into the established marital trap of becoming carbon copies of each other. In pattern breaking, although the goal is a common and uniting one, the challenging events of every moment require a very personal response. And in the process, each spouse develops along his or her very individual lines. Marital mates who look forward together to nothing more exciting than the evening news on television not only become less interesting to each other in that vapid environment but also find that they honestly can't generate new and original thoughts, and that they have difficulty making important decisions. Their growth has come to a halt, and mental stagnation is part of the total picture. Their entertainment is all outside of their own efforts. And soon, as joint spectators of the same show, their idling minds are locked into the same track, and even their arguments begin to sound like a well-rehearsed stage routine. On the other hand, pattern-breaking couples, whose entertainment arises from unusual situations that require every ounce of their input, have a very personal response to these occasions, and over a period of time proceed to develop the newly discovered abilities that have emerged. With vibrant patterns there is no possibility of becoming carbon copies of each other. In fact one partner can seldom, if ever, predict what the other will come up with in order to deal with the variety of happenings that are an integral part of new life-styles.

The adventurers in Puerto Rico, Bob and Enid, are good examples of two Pattern Breakers who became more united while struggling for the same goal, yet who developed as individuals—the reason that they began to sincerely enjoy each other's company. Bob was surprised to see the person who had been a dull companion suddenly change into a resourceful Pattern Breaker who did remarkably well within the context of a new culture, while Enid found herself looking forward to being with this changed person who adventured daily into the Spanish-speaking marketplace.

Pattern-breaking marrieds don't sit around waiting for new signs of physical and mental stagnation and decline in each other. And they don't pay any attention to those reams of jokes that deal with the supposedly funny breakdowns of mind and body after the age of forty or fifty. This pattern of enjoyment of the robust sight of each other is a major dividend, stemming from their new life-styles. Only the young in spirit and body can meet the demands of a challenging mode, and what a joy it is to see one's companion of many years act half his or her age, and in the process look a lot younger, too. If activities determine our effective age and also decide, to a large degree, the features of our personalities, then new life-modes can only bring a whole new vista to the marriage framework, with each partner fully expecting the other to continue growing and changing. In a demanding mode there's really no choice; the participants have to grow, change, stay young, and stay healthy.

At a social gathering a sixtyish woman who went on occasional day-sails with her husband but who had successfully resisted his efforts to live on their comfortable sloop, said to me, "I just can't imagine living on a boat . . . mainly because a boat is simply no place to be sick!" Since I knew she wasn't suffering from any chronic ailment, I couldn't resist answering, "Yes, and that's precisely why people who live on boats are seldom sick!" Too comfortable a life makes it too easy to succumb to the expected forms of decline: to move about slowly, to ride in a car whenever possible, to give in to the first sign of malaise—in short to fall into a pattern of failing health wherein husband and wife must go along propping each other up, rather than enjoying each other's company to the fullest. In our demanding life aboard Romany Star, whenever we feel "something coming on," our first reaction is, we can't get sick . . . someone's got to sail the boat. We have to walk considerable distances for provisions because there's no way to fit even the smallest wheeled-vehicle onto our thirty-eight-foot sailboat, and we're often in places where paid transportation is difficult to obtain. We expect each other to face up to the various requirements of the life we have chosen. And the eight years we have had under these conditions have been the most physically and mentally active of our lives. We are convinced that these years could not have been so fine in a less-demanding setting.

The domestic scene can be incredibly harmonious when a couple is breaking patterns. Usually, what appear to be inbred reasons for marital fights and squabbles are actually products of the old, boring, and irritating settings. In the new ambience the irritants are absent, and there's no good reason for fighting. Disagreements, in our experience, are of a concrete nature—dealing with how to handle a particular situation—rather than the nagging emotional upsets that come from not having anything important toward which to direct one's energies. If one of us is pressed to the point of exploding, which sometimes happens, the target is the crisis that has developed, not one of the two people aboard. And when the solution is found, there are no personal hurts to be ironed out—only a lot of shared joy that the emergency has been dealt with successfully.

In a sense a pattern-breaking couple resembles a pair of sol-diers who are waging a battle—a happy battle, that is—for a mutually beneficial cause. They hang in together despite the defeats and find each other's company absolutely essential when it's time for the victory celebrations. Married people who have kept each other's morale up during a difficult academic course know how rewarding those days can be—all the way from the hard times of study to the time when the grades, good or bad, are handed out and the jubilant or deflated emotions are shared with someone who understands the problems that were faced. The same is true, for example, of the couple who sweat out the requirements for learning to pilot a small plane, who establish an innovative kind of business that demands every drop of their know-how and strength, or who go full-time into the creative arts, even though a step down the economic ladder is involved.

Mental fatigue, that enemy of our life force that too often man-ages to put its evil stamp on longtime marriages, just can't survive the interesting happenings in the lives of serious Pattern Breakers. With all of society pouring out a message to the effect that anyone over forty should be getting tired of living, it takes a marathon effort—such as a wholehearted break away from the old patterns—to keep from sinking into mental doldrums. Making matters worse, that lazy streak that runs through most of us can easily find indulgence in the world's acceptance of our slowing down. It is all too easy to settle for less than best and to put the blame on age, when the truth of the matter is that we are as capable as ever and only need to get into meaningful activity. Anyone who has dealt successfully with a slothful state of mind can attest to the fact that although mental fatigue produces physical fatigue, it is also true that stimulating ventures wipe out mental fatigue, and con-sequently physical fatigue. The retired couple who rely on shop-ping malls and a limited circle of friends for their entertainment should not be surprised when they often feel too tired to even get into the car or invite someone over for dinner. As the mind slows down, life slows down in every sense. And the married relationship—that delicate balance of strength and weakness—is the first to feel the slackening.

Niles and Vera, a couple of retirees who were tired of living and, it follows, of each other, were literally picked up by the seat of their pants and plopped down into a new pattern that saved their marriage. In a windfall kind of property trade—begun and consummated practically overnight—they ended up, as part of the deal, with a German shepherd–breeding business that couldn't be sold until a lot of improvements were made. They had owned and exhibited German shepherds but had never dreamed of becoming professional breeders. A move to another city was involved, as well as an in-depth study of bloodlines; breeding, birthing, and nutritional procedures; and management problems and registration rules. As they were forced to become active, their minds came alive, their old energy returned, and their new marriage pattern outshone anything they had ever experienced.

Chronologically older marrieds who lead pattern-breaking lives are a source of wonderment to those around them. Since they just don't fit into the usual mold, with their energy and youthfully expectant attitudes, they elicit a treatment that is far different from what is usually dealt out to people their age. And all of this heaps more fuel onto their inner fire. Instead of seeing waning human beings reflected in the mirror of other people's treatment of them, they see themselves as worthy of admiration, and this sight can only add to their determination to remain that way.

In the early days of our sailing life, when we had been married for a quarter of a century, we spent a weekend at the dock, polishing our new twenty-six-foot sloop Prana, lounging in the cockpit, and generally feeling good about our new personalities as sailors—although at that point, we had still not gathered the courage to venture out without the help of experienced friends. We felt like two teenagers with a marvelous new toy and spent a lot of time just holding hands and concocting fantasies about the grand adventures we were going to have. A middle-age man, alone on a motor vessel next to us, also appeared to be spending the weekend at the dock, and as time progressed, we began to exchange

boat-to-boat pleasantries with him, never getting around to intro-
ducing ourselves and actually getting to know him. A week or so
later, one of our sailing friends who, it developed, knew our dockside neighbor well approached us on the street, grinning from ear
to ear.

"Guess what!" he said, chuckling. "My old friend Joe, who
owns the boat next to you at the marina, asked me if I knew the
newlyweds who spent the weekend on Prana!"

We all got a good laugh out of the twenty-five-year mistake,
and, best of all, our marital self-image received a rejuvenating
shot in the arm. We would like to think that if history could repeat
itself and Joe's first glimpse of us could occur today, thirteen years
later, his calculation would still be as far off base.

When couples are engaged in vital life-styles, they not only
have the pleasure of seeing what they're doing reflected in the
eyes of others but also benefit in a big way from constant exposure
to a lot of people who are leading thrilling lives. Since age is no
factor among adventurers, family friends run the gamut from
chronologically young to old, and inspiration can be gained from
all of them. A rather dramatic juxtaposition of ages occurred
recently at one of our favorite anchorages. The weather had been
disturbed for a while, and leaving a bay that was choppy and
windswept, we headed for one of the British Virgin Islands' most
peaceful havens, Trellis Bay, off the coast of Beef Island. After
dropping our anchor, we straightened up the exterior of the boat
and then went inside for a cool drink. The noisy clanking of chain
through the hatches told us that we were getting neighbors on
both sides, and as soon as our thirst was quenched, we returned
to the cockpit to check out the "neighborhood." To our starboard a
couple who appeared to be in their early twenties were furling a
worn-looking mainsail onto the boom of a small vessel whose bat-
tered paint job gave a hint of some long, hard traveling. On our
port a late-sixtyish couple were erecting a spiffy-looking canopy
over their immaculate forty-foot yawl. Tom got into the dinghy
and motored over to invite all four newcomers to Romany Star for
sundowners.

Rick and Sally, Australians, were twenty-four years old and only a week before had sailed into the Virgin Islands from a trip that had originated in Darwin two years before. They regaled us with colorful tales of their trip through the Indian Ocean, their long stay in Africa, their trip to Brazil (where, owing to lack of previously obtained visas, they had been forced to leave after only a week), and their sail up the South American coast to Venezuela and finally to the Virgins through the Windward and Leeward chains. They had lived on their boat for six years—earning money by obtaining a wide variety of jobs in different ports—and they had decided to continue their sail in the direction of the Panama Canal, through the Pacific and back home again, where they would buy a small farm and would produce, along with the usual crops, a family of five children. When the quintet became old enough to help crew a boat, they would all seven set sail together.

Paul and Jennie, a lively pair of sexagenarians from England, had worked in the chartering business "down island" for fifteen years, running one of the big, traditional, wooden schooners that convey guests up and down the windy, rambunctious seas off the coasts of Grenada, St. Lucia, and Martinique.

"This is our retirement cottage," they laughed, motioning toward their newly purchased vessel, but the plans they proceeded to detail had nothing to do with retirement in the usual sense of the word. Paul and Jennie were genuine Recommencers. Within a year they planned to sail over to England for visits with friends and relatives, and their next trip would be back to the Caribbean en route to the canal and the Pacific. It was clear to see that their "cottage" was going to be in constant motion.

We spent a great evening listening to the riveting projections of two couples who were at opposite ends of the chronological age spectrum but who, in terms of interest and vitality, were meeting squarely in the middle of life. Best of all, from the ambitious plans that were being described, it was obvious that all four of our guests would be lifelong recipients of the rejuvenating benefits that come from setting new marriage patterns. All week long we worked around our boats, and together dived for conch, snor-keled, hiked down the road for provisions, and enjoyed the company of other travelers who sailed into the anchorage. The varying challenges, activities, and people combined to ensure that this life-style we had chosen was still far from becoming the trap that some of the most promising new patterns can be.

THIRTEEN

NEW LIFE-STYLES CAN BE TRAPS, TOO

Sue and Alan, former neighbors of ours, took the first giant step toward fulfilling a lifelong dream when, in their mid-sixties, they sold their home in the Ohio town where they had lived all their lives and moved to the warm weather and semitropical lushness of Miami. Since their economic resources were modest, they purchased a small residence in one of those interdependent communities where everyone is living on a shoestring—such as young couples just beginning a family, retirees who have managed to save enough to escape the clutches of cold weather, immigrants getting a start in the New World, struggling artists. Although Sue and Alan were from the outset reserved in their contacts with people in the neighborhood, Tom and I put the kids to bed early one evening and went over with a little welcoming speech. We were surprised to find that they had some interesting involvements to share: he had been a stamp collector for many years and seemed to enjoy talking about his hobby, and she was skilled in several kinds of handicrafts, samples of which were displayed throughout the house. Both enjoyed music, and they had assembled an impressive collection of the old-time band records.

Over the months a number of their neighbors tried hard to draw the newcomers out of their tight little cocoon, but the two appeared determined to conduct their lives in Miami along the same general lines that life up north had followed. Their only social partners were a couple from their Ohio hometown who had settled in a nearby suburb, and the quartet would get together for cards or dinner two or three times a week in the setting that Sue and Alan had transported *in toto* from their former residence—lace curtains, wool rugs, heavy, dark furniture—or at the other couple's home, which we believed must have been something of a carbon copy. No one was shocked when a few scant months after starting what could have been a new pattern, with their hibiscus hedges and trellised alemandras just beginning to get a good hold on life, our stubborn neighbors announced that they were moving back to their old neighborhood in Ohio.

"We get lonely here," Sue said. "We're used to being with a lot of people."

As soon as they could obtain a reasonable offer from a real estate agent, they shipped their wool rugs, lace curtains, and heavy, dark furniture back up north and left the failed dreamhouse—where just across the street lived a talented, amusing musician of the old school who played in a band at a Miami Beach hotel and who could be spotted most mornings at four o'clock, in elegant white tuxedo, quietly watering his lawn. Also in this neighborhood, just beyond the couple's backyard, resided a warm-hearted pair in their sixties who doted on children and loved to watch auto racing and who could be seen on almost any day playing some inventive game with one of the neighborhood progeny; and on one side of the fledgling hibiscus hedge reigned a remarkable Cuban lady, who was so proud of her first home in the United States that she kept it as resplendent with new paint and pampered shrubbery as a sheik's palace; on the other side lived an Italian couple who loved to cook and were constantly conveying hot pastries to nearby houses, including Sue and Alan's. Furthermore, just a few doors down the street resided a talented young carpenter who made a point of visiting everyone in the unhappy newcomers' block, offering his gratuitous services for repairing those many flaws that can develop in low-cost housing. And at the risk of belaboring the point, I must include the fact that in this remarkable community, whoever had a car at his or her disposal was always glad to jam it full of one-car-family people who were marooned at home, needing rides into town or to the local supermarket. For the taker it was a splendid neighborhood. But for the closed-minded Ohio couple it became a self-devised trap. And unfortunately, the same thing happens to pseudo–Pattern Breakers such as Sue and Alan all over the world—even in the most exotic of settings.

Bruce and Rosalind were among the first people we met after sailing into Antigua's quaint English Harbour. Short on provisions, we hurried by taxi to the island's most complete food store, and when our cart was well loaded, began a conversation with the touristy-looking pair of Americans while waiting in line with them at the cash register. To their surprise, I believe, we immediately invited them to Romany Star for evening drinks; the next day they invited us to their hilltop home, and thus the four of us began a relationship that was kept going over the next five years by occasional letters and several more visits to Antigua. A high point of our trips into English Harbour was the Pennsylvania couple's generous invitation for hot showers and dinner. While we were on the island, we always managed to get together a number of times aboard Romany Star or at their comfortable, flower-surrounded residence, which overlooked a gorgeous ocean view. Much of our time in Antigua was spent in doing the sort of exploring we prefer: getting to know Antiguans, telling them about our experiences and in return learning about their colorful backgrounds as fishermen or farmers. It didn't take us long to find out that our new friends didn't share our interest in the island.

Roz and Bruce had started spending vacations in Antigua while they were still enmeshed in the working life, and they had eventually begun the slow process of building a home there, with the plan of moving into it upon retirement. Principally, they liked the island for its climate and beaches, and—we were astounded to discover—in the many years they had vacationed and lived there, they had never become socially involved with anyone from the native population. Their friends were people like themselves. It was clear that none in this tight little group had any desire to know anything about the people whose roots ran far back into the exotic, and sometimes thorny, past of the Caribbean. We noticed that Roz and Bruce weren't even interested in the droves of boaters from all over the world who make their way to the enviable shelter of English Harbour; after all, we were the ones who had taken the initiative at the food market. Their shopping forays—as nonverbal as these trips were—constituted the couple's only outreach from an otherwise-sheltered life, and as Roz said on our very first meeting, "This place can get boring!"

But sadly (in view of their oblivious condition), there was a life to be shared and an astonishing story to be heard at every hand. The eighty-two-year-old man who dispensed their gasoline had been a fisherman back in the primitive days of the island and was full of accounts of nearly being swamped at sea, of how he used to build the sturdy wooden boats that were the typical craft of those long-ago days, of his family's hard and good times—all so different from a Statesider's experience. It was fascinating to sit with him on Romany Star and try to see Antigua through his eyes. The owner of the food store where we had met our unadventuresome friends turned out to be the son of a farming couple who despite Antigua's frequent droughts had managed to market enough produce to give him an excellent education. In their eighties, they were still living on their farm, and we were overwhelmed by their generosity, displayed in lavish gifts of fruits and vegetables and some of the most delicious, spicy dinners we've ever partaken of. Their stories of the old days in Antigua kept us at rapt attention for hours at a time. Everywhere one would turn, there were people who—after their initial reserve had been penetrated—were ready with an offer of friendship that was outstanding for its sincerity and total commitment.

Roz and Bruce eventually found that swimming at the beach and socializing with their limited circle of acquaintances fell short of making them happy. After all that elaborate groundwork of erecting a home and making the big move, they forfeited their opportunity to become genuine Recommencers, sold the beautiful residence that had become more of a trap than a pleasure, and joined the ranks of retirees they had known all their lives back in their Pennsylvania hometown.

A move to a new city or to a foreign country provides the most propitious of settings for breaking old patterns and establishing new ones; despite this fact, however, a lot of people who do their pattern breaking right at home are more successful than some of the travelers. The Maryland couple who are breaking patterns every day at their auto service center are good examples; through their customers from far-flung places, they have found an ever-new route to effective pattern breaking. For true-blue adventurers of this nature, local folks are interesting, too—those with varied ethnic and economic backgrounds, or maybe even the people next door who, for the asking, have inspiring stories and lives to share. Pattern breaking appears to boil down to a very internal situation, best described as a mind-set toward life; the person who is open to, and interested in, new experiences and people can break patterns on a daily basis and establish new life-styles at will, right in the setting of his or her hometown, while the closed-minded pseudo–Pattern Breaker can journey to Timbuktu, never break any important patterns, and end up in a lot of personally designed traps.

Examples of travelers who fall into traps can be found in the RV-er who begins to find it too difficult to get on the road again and starts spending too much time in one place, or in contrast the RV-er who falls into the common pattern of dashing from place to place and never delving into the gems of human nature and natural surroundings along the way. In a trap, too, are the sailor who "touches base" with countries and islands in a feverish urge to effect long voyages, and the traveler who decides to "do the world" by living in different countries a few months at a time, establishes residence and sees the points of interest that are listed in the guidebooks, but doesn't make a sincere effort to tie into the local point of view and to form true and lasting relationships.

Adventurers who establish new life-styles on old, familiar

ground must be, however, the most alert of all Pattern Breakers. Not only can their new life-styles become traps, but also the tangible and intangible features of the former traps are still right on the scene, waiting to ensnare their unwary old tenants. The recently adopted modes—with the accompanying new habits and attitudes—have to be potent ones in order to survive. "It isn't fair to my family" and "I'm needed at home" are timeworn excuses for a mother's leaving full-time study, when the truth is that home and family will usually benefit far more from her pattern-breaking example than from having dinner on the table at the same hour every evening. Other examples of erring home-ground adventurers are those who start new and novel businesses, lose sight of the "grail," and begin to envy those nine-to-five friends and to long for the undemanding old jobs, forgetting how boring those days were. Daily reaffirmation of the goal, combined with a hard look at the negative vibes that are doing the damage, will go a long way in helping Pattern Breakers to keep that same enthusiastic attitude they had on the very first day of their ventures.

Life-styles with a number of built-in subpatterns afford an opportunity for constant change and challenge, but even the most varied modes can turn into traps. When Tom and I began living aboard, we were continually faced with challenge as we struggled to outfit our boat in a relatively underdeveloped area and, when our outfitting was completed, as we took our first long trip "down-island." Our activities during the years since have also been demanding and full of interest. As we have traveled, however, we have observed a number of live-aboard subpatterns that, were we to indulge in them, would not provide us with enough challenge to keep life properly "spiced up." For instance, we have known people who spend most of their time anchored in the same favorite bay; others who live at docks and in a large sense are land dwellers who, as we see it, would be better off in a comfortable apartment; some who have favorite trips, such as from the British Virgin Islands to St. Martin, which they undertake on a regular basis, seldom departing from that familiar track. There seem to be a variety of subpatterns in personal relationships, too, such as sailors who relate mainly to other sailors, some who opt to forgo friends drawn from their own category and instead attach themselves almost exclusively to the townspeople, and others who withdraw into the privacy of their boats and eschew the company of one and all.

Since moving onto Romany Star we have enjoyed a number of subpatterns, such as researching—through study as well as by tracking down and talking with experienced people—setups that can add to our comfort (solar cells, for instance); sampling the feeling of setting up residence in a particularly nice bay (being careful not to let the experiment become a habit); getting into community activities in various areas where we are anchored. A repetitive subpattern has been our tuning into the local business community, through Tom's occasional employment; this can be a real eye-opener as to area politics and the working person's problems.

Although we have teetered on the edge of a number of subpattern traps, we have so far managed to regain our balance in time. Our most common temptation is the peaceful bay where the anchor never needs to be checked during the night; this is fine for marginal or bad weather, but under usual conditions one can find a plethora of bays where, with a bit of vigilance, some outstanding natural wonders can be safely enjoyed. Tom's business interests once threw out a net that could have entrapped us for too long at a marina, but we reviewed our priorities and set sail again. A subpattern that combines sailing with part-time house-sitting—in some outstanding residences with impressive views—is a siren call that we thus far have chosen to ignore; we haven't wanted to leave the freedom of our life afloat. Perhaps someday we'll try that tempting combination of land and sea; after all, that's half of what pattern breaking is all about—keeping an open mind to any healthful change. The other half—making sure that one doesn't fall into the velvet trap of routine—would turn house-sitting in a cushy tropical setting into a real challenge.

Many Pattern Breakers who start their own businesses have a good opportunity for keeping their lives full of excitement through the creation of subpatterns. Often one subpattern will generate another, and the resultant innovation can become an unending affair. A good example of someone who took advantage of subpatterns is Theta, a talented ceramicist who started out as a hobbyist, then began to teach neighbors in a little workshop she developed in her downstairs den, and went on to make elegant ceramic planters for businesses, such as for merchandise distributors who sent expensive gifts to their best clients. She volunteered to fill these ceramic pieces with appropriate plants—for a price—and in the process decided that ceramics and plants were a natural duo. Her next step was to open a full-fledged business with a ceramics workshop attached to a plant nursery; she sold plants and the tasteful handmade pieces both separately and in combination. This enterprising woman has a number of future innovations lined up, including a ceramics class for very small children. Her involvement in subpatterns guarantees that she will never fall into the life-style trap.

A couple we know who entered the health food business have kept their lives challenging through constant innovation. Their venture was pattern breaking at the outset, since their community did not offer a large clientele for health food. The ambitious pair decided to open a restaurant-store combination, with the restaurant serving natural foods in gourmet style, in an informal yet tasteful setting. Customers in this charming place are of all kinds of food persuasion, and the dishes are so delectable that the health motive becomes secondary to outright enjoyment. Shopping in the store can be done at any time—before eating (purchases are kept behind the counter), in the interim between ordering and waiting to be served, or at the end of the meal. A worthwhile subpattern is the regular sponsorship of health seminars; although this couple definitely does not belong to that irritating breed of people who wear one out with lectures on vitamins and sea vegetables, the two do enjoy offering information for interested clients. Struggling musicians, poets, and actors offer a variety of entertainment and are a "pet project" of the owners. Another subpattern is the couple's involvement in national organizations that deal with diet-related issues. We were once regular patrons of their store-restaurant and were amazed by the constant improvements in decor, menu, and selling approaches. Everyone was benefiting from this eclectic life-style; customers always experienced an entertaining, healthy evening, and the owners—charged up with new plans and experiments—were immersed in a life mode that was not only exciting but also financially rewarding. It is impossible to imagine these two as victims of a life-style trap.

Many very sincere Pattern Breakers get snagged in the wrong life-style and for lack of imagination have a hard time working their way out; in fact a large number just flatly give up. Ted, who loved working on motors, lived in an unzoned area at the city's outskirts, where it was possible to conduct a business out of his home. Upon recommencement he decided to go into the repair of a variety of small motors, such as those used in lawn mowers, edgers, and equipment for vegetable gardening. Some big problems soon surfaced. Ted's thirty-year job career had been behind a desk in an accounting office, with very little contact with the public, and to his despair he discovered that the public relations aspect of his repair service was decidedly not up his alley; disgruntled customers drove him up the wall. His wife wasn't interested in participating in the business, and the financial potential wasn't good enough to warrant employing someone, so Ted took the easy way out and didn't even try to find a solution or another interesting pattern. He closed the business he had looked forward to during those office-bound years and changed from enthusiastic Recommencer to bored retiree.

In contrast Jena and Giles, who recommenced to a small farm after having owned a successful grocery business, turned what could have been a trap into the route to a vital way of life. Although they had always thought that they would like to return to the setting in which they had grown up—that of the small, independent farmer—they found that tilling the soil, even with the best of equipment, was not for them. They had noticed that the farmers in their area nearly always had food go to waste. Their mental wheels started turning, and they quit farming and established an attractive highwayside market where this good produce could be sold. Jena had become interested in quilting, and she set up an area adjacent to the vegetable bins, where women in their seventies and eighties, who had been quilting since childhood, could give demonstrations and sell their creations to the passing tourist trade. This clever couple have no regrets about having failed as farmers; if they hadn't, they would never have experienced the outstanding success of their present venture.

There is a mesmerizing quality to life aboard a sailboat—the constant rocking motion, the smell of salt water, the rhythmic patterns of seabirds as they soar and dip for their darting prey. And we fully realize that our own magic carpet in this hypnotic realm, Romany Star, can either become a trap that keeps us from realizing a number of challenging plans we have in mind or can be a springboard to their fulfillment. Since boat maintenance, a steady stream of new people, and travel to distant ports provide an always-varied life, it is no wonder that many Pattern Breakers continue to find challenge in a lifelong, all-involving commitment to the sea. Personalities are different, however, and there are as many complete definitions of pattern breaking as there are people. The crew of Romany Star, whose definitions of pattern breaking agree on some of the major points, have a burning desire not only to pursue a life at sea but also to do a number of things that don't include boating. An in-depth exploration of the United States by RV will be next on our agenda, and we would like to drive all the way up to Alaska. After a span of time back aboard Romany Star, we plan to set off again—this time to a foreign country, where we will live as full-fledged land-dwelling people in a small-town environment, making friends with the local citizens and learning about their customs. Since we firmly reject sailing in cold weather, and since boat travel too often offers knowledge of only the coastal areas of countries—because of the necessity of keeping an eye on one's boat—the best plan for us seems to be to travel by air and to live in a rented room or apartment. This experience, combined with a wintertime stay on Romany Star in warm-weather areas, will be repeated many times, in a number of countries. And other activities, such as raising our own food, will be worked in along the way.

As a springboard Romany Star offers the possibility of a few days' work to store her ashore on wooden chocks, with another few days' efforts to put her back in the water. There's no electricity to turn off, no pipes to insulate against freezing, paper delivery to be stopped, or grass to be mowed while we're gone. We can throw our things in a soft bag, walk out of the storage yard, and hop a plane to new adventures, with the comfortable knowledge that our floating home is in safekeeping until our return. But as much as we love her, if our springboard ever becomes a life-style trap, we'll sell her without a qualm. If life becomes dull and routine and we're tempted to admit that we're feeling the impact of aging, there'll be no doubt as to the fact that it's time to make a change. But as long as every day is exciting and challenging, as long as what we're doing keeps us young and healthy, with life continuing to be remarkably fine, we won't have to go searching for the right pattern . . . we'll know that we're squarely in the middle of it.

FOURTEEN

INSIDE THE
PATTERN BREAKER

The people we meet usually ask us how we came to live on a thirty-eight-foot sailboat. Along with the details of how we opted for life afloat, our explanation almost always includes the fact that when we set out on our adventure, we sold or gave away the tangible acquisitions of a lifetime: residence, the family silver, furniture, bibelots, and a lot of assorted junk—in short everything that didn't fit into our usual new pattern. This facet of our pattern-breaking experience seems to be as shocking as the fact of our unorthodox life mode . . . at times, even more shocking. Although this "unloading"—for us a liberating event— does not have to be imitated by every Pattern Breaker, it is safe to say that all true adventurers will do a lot of things that will be equally as unsettling for their family and friends. And in the process they'll find that some radical shifts are taking place in the way they're viewing the world.

Like many people Tom and I were rabid accumulators, and consequently, our closets, cabinets, and drawers were stuffed with such important items as an instrument for making florets out of radishes, six different kinds of "hot curl" mechanisms, enough unmatched drinking glasses to serve libations to the entire United Nations assembly, a five-year supply of bags for the very first vacuum cleaner we had owned, along with stacks of framed prints and paintings that in our lifetime would not find room in our crowded wall space—in other words the typical American home collection. Until the day we decided to move aboard Romany Star, our mad purchasing continued at full swing, with few things making us happier than to stagger out of a shopping mall beneath loads of packages full of items to add to the burgeoning stacks, rows, and piles that awaited us at home.

A year after we had made our big leap into a new life, we took a trip back to the States, and since shopping malls are a major modern-day diversion, Roy, the friend in whose home we were visiting, took us on a Saturday outing to one of the country's largest and most beautiful centers. After touring at least a dozen stores brimful of every kind of merchandise imaginable, with no stops at a cash register, Roy turned to us and in a rather tight voice inquired, "Haven't you seen anything you'd like to buy?"

Tom's reply, "There doesn't seem to be anything we can use," almost put Roy over the edge, but rallying, he said, pointing, "Well, there's a different kind of store over there, and I frankly have never been able to find a single thing in it, but if you want to see it, go ahead . . . I'll meet you outside in ten minutes."

The "different kind of store" proved to be a godsend for us, offering such indispensable items as a large magnet that can be tied to a string and lowered into deep places (including water) to retrieve lost objects; a miniature battery-driven fan that can be wedged into cramped spots where a worker really needs some cool air; a rustproof, manually operated eggbeater; a toaster that can be used over a gas flame; a flashlight that can be fastened onto the head, leaving hands free to do various repairs. Thirty minutes into what had become for us an all-out shopping spree, Roy tracked us down, hunched over a terrific find. To our plea, "Could we shop awhile longer?" he scratched his head and said, "I'll be damned!" When we returned to his house that evening, his wife, Jill, managed to control her amazement enough to say a few nice things about our odd assortment of purchases; however, she couldn't resist asking, "But did you go through Bloomingdale's?"

Later Jill took me to one side and in a woman-to-woman voice said, "Now you can tell me the truth . . . you miss all those nice things you used to have, don't you?" Jill had known us during that three-decade-long series of carefully decorated houses and apartments with their efficient kitchens, generous plumbing, and space . . . yes, above all, space. Her question didn't entirely miss its mark; I knew what she was talking about, for I hadn't been oblivious during our tour of the shopping mall to the rows of king-size and queen-size and everything but boat-bunk-size beds, the elegant sofas and chairs into which the body can properly sink, and the multitude of items that are too irrelevant, fragile, and/or expensive to consign to a vessel that rises and falls and leans precariously as it makes its way through twelve-foot seas. I didn't have to mull over my answer, however.

"No," I replied—gently, because I didn't want to appear to be condemning our friends' life-style—"I don't miss a single thing. If all those goodies could be a part of what we're doing, then I guess I'd miss them, but the way we see it, the kind of life we're leading now is too good to even begin to compare it with the old days when we had all the luxuries."

My answer wasn't just a result of having lived aboard for a year; in foundation it dated back to our initial decision to adopt a new pattern. We had been happy to rid ourselves of any hindrance to our new life-style for the simple fact that the moment we accepted the freedom to live as we wanted, all our old attitudes were instantaneously shaken loose. Day-to-day fulfillment and enjoyment began to take top priority, and a trade-off for luxury and comfort wasn't even worthy of consideration. In fact from our vantage point now, outside the framework of the way most people live, we are astonished at the sacrifices people will make in the name of comfort—for example, when they continue to work at jobs they despise in order to afford luxuries or to suffer total boredom rather than make the effort necessary for finding excitement. This new mental freedom has opened up a world of possibilities for us, none of which include voluntarily consigning the precious days of our lives to anything less than what we consider to be the best.

Mental freedom is a potent emotion, and although adventurers often flabbergast their observers with the inventive life modes they choose to adopt, the most awesome part of all is the change that freedom is bringing about inside the Pattern Breaker. It's no news that society is reluctant to endorse "free souls," preferring that everyone follow a set pattern, thereby—supposedly—making life more peaceful for all concerned. But Pattern Breakers refuse to buy that preference. Through their own experience they have learned that freedom of thought results in an open mind toward situations and people, and that when situations and people are viewed as they really are, understanding—and solutions—will naturally result.

Emergence into freedom of thought affects every action and attitude existent in the lives of Pattern Breakers. Ways of thinking that at one time met with outright rejection are now given their "day in court." Newborn adventurers realize that if they could have been so wrong about what they formerly thought was the best way to conduct their lives, they must also have been wrong concerning at least some of the philosophies they opposed. Before our recommencement Tom and I had always considered ourselves to be more open minded than most of the people we knew. We realize now, however, that there were many subjects that we adamantly refused to explore. Among our friends were some unusual personalities, such as struggling painters and musicians and a number of people with offbeat credos, but in truth, although we enjoyed those relationships and as a rule opened our ears to what one and all had to say, we too often failed to open our minds to the possibility of believing what we were hearing.

"We aren't gullible," we would say to each other, not realizing that gullibility can also apply to people who meekly obey the brainwashers' proclamation that "way-out" thoughts shouldn't be given careful consideration.

It is interesting to note that one always remembers society's rebels, whereas the dull people are easy to forget. Whenever I think of rebels we have known, a happening that took place long before our pattern-breaking days flashes into my mind. Every detail is clear. The setting is the living room of our condominium apartment, with its comfortable furnishings and orderly appearance. Tom and I are dressed in our conservative slacks-and-top attire for at-home gatherings, and opposite us, perched on the sofa, is a diminutive, fortyish woman who had once been a teacher in the high school in which I was also employed. In this scene Sheena is attired in faded jeans, a tie-dyed knit shirt, and scuffed thong sandals, and on the rug beside her feet is a lumpy duffel bag, which apparently contains everything she has needed in the way of garments for the past year. She has been backpacking in Central America, working as an English-language typist when her funds would get low, and the question that seems to bug me most of all is, What in the world did she wear on the job? As a teacher her attire could have been accurately described as arresting—serapes, brilliant scarves, peasant skirts, thongs . . . always thongs. And she was regularly being reprimanded by our principal, who was light on academics and heavy on discipline and smooth operation of all systems, for staying at school till dark in order to help failing or highly motivated students.

Though invited, Sheena wasn't planning to stay with us; she had announced right off that she was going to bunk with a dozen or so friends who lived in a big, old house on the city's outskirts. I had mentally noted, a commune—where she'll no doubt be smoking pot and doing all the other questionable things that hippies do. As I mused further over this talented teacher's manifest degeneration, she began to enthusiastically describe a health food diet she had begun, and in the process dropped the bombshell that her next travel stop would be an institute in the Northeast where the subject of macrobiotics was being taught as a preventative, and sometimes cure, of tumors and cysts.

"I have a number of cysts here," she said, pressing her breasts in an uninhibited fashion. "I've had a biopsy and they aren't malignant."

"Why don't you have surgery?" I asked.

"I really don't think it's necessary," she answered, and at that moment my idling mind closed tightly shut to any further idea this obviously fanatical woman might offer. Since that day, of course, medical research has shown a relationship between breast cysts and diet, and Sheena's approach, though still not completely accepted in medical circles, has been somewhat vindicated. The medical aspects of the encounter in our apartment aren't what make it stand out in my memory, however; rather, I am aghast at how firmly I closed my mental doors to even considering the possibility that Sheena could be correct.

Since breaking patterns, I have often thought of Sheena and of other similar rebels, i.e., Pattern Breakers, who passed through our lives during those prerecommencement days. Few matched her creative appearance—in fact most of them looked quite ordinary—but there was an unmistakable similarity in their approach to life. At the time, we were not visibly influenced by any of that passing parade; we were spectators who heard some unique bits of creative thinking or got a few laughs from all those peculiar lifestyles. But now we realize that the profligate example of mental freedom that was offered by the lives of those Pattern Breakers was causing reverberations that eventually would reach and affect our personal moment of decision. We feel grateful to all the Sheenas who played a role in our departure from the beaten track.

The changes that take place in the Pattern Breaker's mind-set make living a day at a time not only easy but in reality an integral part of the new life-style. The uptight attitudes about having to perform in a certain way tomorrow are replaced by a flexible outlook: Since I don't have to adhere to any fixed pattern, I will meet tomorrow with whatever approach is called for at that time. Recommencers aren't the only beneficiaries of this efficient way of thought; all Pattern Breakers feel the good results of living each day according to a plan that is right for the existent circumstances, instead of according to a plan that was formulated during a time when no one could possibly have known what the next day would bring. This flexible attitude, another result of the mental freedom that is enjoyed by Pattern Breakers, is illustrated in the life of a sailor we met—an Englishman who set out five years ago to travel around the world. He voyaged from his native land to the Caribbean, the logical first lap of a circumnavigation, and to people who inquire as to when he's taking off again, he always replies, "I'm actually on my way right now." He is earning good money as a marine surveyor, and while fattening the kitty for further travels, is having a lot of fun in what many consider to be an unparalleled sailing ground. Even if he never moves on, right now he's living and enjoying a day at a time. And for this intelligent Pattern Breaker, that's all that matters. In addition he's living proof that pattern breaking is a very personal, internal matter.

One of the most salient consequences of mental freedom is its effect on personal values. What was of earth-shattering importance during the old days suddenly seems trifling, and with this phenomenon a whole new set of values begins to emerge. Among the Pattern Breakers we have known there has been a consistent thread that can be spotted throughout this reshuffling of values: a greater importance is attached to human relationships. People, and time spent with people, outrank all other considerations. On the pattern-breaking scene we have witnessed some incredible acts of person-to-person help. For example, it isn't at all uncommon for sailors to place their own safety and vessels in jeopardy in order to go to the rescue of grounded or otherwise disabled boats. On land and at sea, ham radio operators are traditional Good Samaritans. On a recent trip to the States we listened to a series of communications (during a nasty snowstorm) that resulted in the rescue of a driver whose car had plunged off a bridge and into an icy river and—during the same time span—the directing of medical aid to a group that had barely survived the crash of their small plane on a rugged mountain slope. A fine example, too, is a Pattern Breaker we have known since the early years of our marriage, a man most people consider to be strange because, though he holds a doctorate in geology, he has never placed importance on earning any money beyond what he needs for a simple, healthy life-style. Almost any visit to his home will reveal some new person he is helping, either physically, with food and lodging, or emotionally. Although helpful people are found everywhere—not solely among the ranks of Pattern Breakers—it has been our experience that the latter group are usually more willing to completely deviate from their normal path in order to lend a hand. Even if they are still employed, their mental freedom allows them to place the needs of others before the preservation of routine. And these helpful people rarely suffer any setback as the result of their generosity; on the contrary they nearly always come out winning in every way.

When values undergo a shift, criticism from others suddenly loses its sting. Since Pattern Breakers are mentally free, the standards imposed by society lose their importance, and all decisions point toward one goal: to be true to one's own personal standards. This doesn't mean that the mind is closed to input; it means that after the open mind has sifted through and carefully studied the available information, it is the thinker, not society, who makes the final decision as to which course of action is the correct one. This rule applies to the spiritual realm, too. Doctrines and beliefs must be sifted through the reliable filter the Creator has allowed each of us to have for the asking: a combination of free mind and spirit. After all, if we had been intended to thoughtlessly accept credos, why were we endowed with that potent mechanism of free choice?

At the same time that outside criticism is losing its sting, Pattern Breakers are, quite unawares, becoming less judgmental of those around them. Actually, it becomes imperative to give others the same freedom of thought and action that they are enjoying. This is all the natural result of their determination to run their own lives; their independence has made them feel remarkably good about themselves, and all those felicitous feelings have a tendency to spill over to other people. And after all, in a world so full of possibilities, isn't there plenty of room for every kind of person? It isn't surprising that the only viable philosophy for this relaxed state of affairs becomes one of live and let live.

Without exception sincere Pattern Breakers will turn into new and different people and will continue to change for as long as they live—a regenerative way of being that keeps them young. The secret behind this constant inner change, with the accompanying rejuvenation, will be all those pattern-breaking activities; departure from the accepted continuum of programmed decline will have set the usual aging processes awry. These brave adventurers won't be perfect; like most avid doers they'll make a lot of mistakes—a fact that won't deter them in the least from forging on. As they take the first giant step toward freedom, a domino effect will begin inside and the old values will topple. New values will fall into place, and happiness will crowd out the old discontent.

Whatever their actions may be as the result of all this inner revolution, Pattern Breakers will stubbornly refuse to fade into a background of routine and monotony; like Sheena they will be—above all—unforgettable.